THE VISUAL
DICTIONARY *of the*
SKELETON

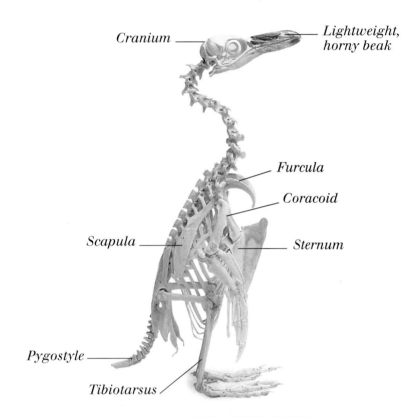

Cranium

Lightweight, horny beak

Furcula

Coracoid

Scapula

Sternum

Pygostyle

Tibiotarsus

PENGUIN SKELETON

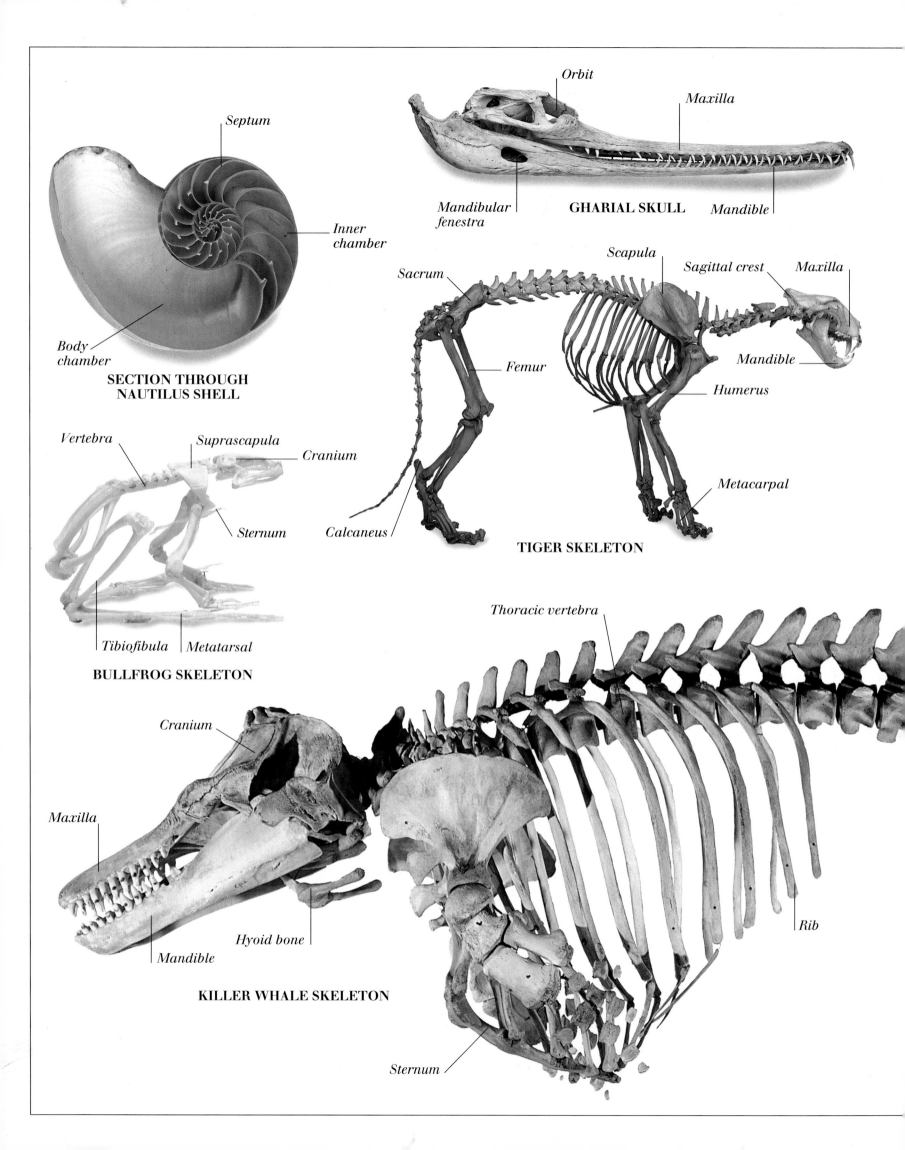

Septum

Inner chamber

Body chamber

SECTION THROUGH NAUTILUS SHELL

Orbit

Maxilla

Mandibular fenestra

GHARIAL SKULL

Mandible

Vertebra

Suprascapula

Cranium

Sternum

Tibiofibula *Metatarsal*

BULLFROG SKELETON

Sacrum

Scapula

Sagittal crest

Maxilla

Femur

Mandible

Humerus

Calcaneus

Metacarpal

TIGER SKELETON

Thoracic vertebra

Cranium

Maxilla

Hyoid bone

Mandible

Rib

Sternum

KILLER WHALE SKELETON

THE VISUAL
DICTIONARY *of the*
SKELETON

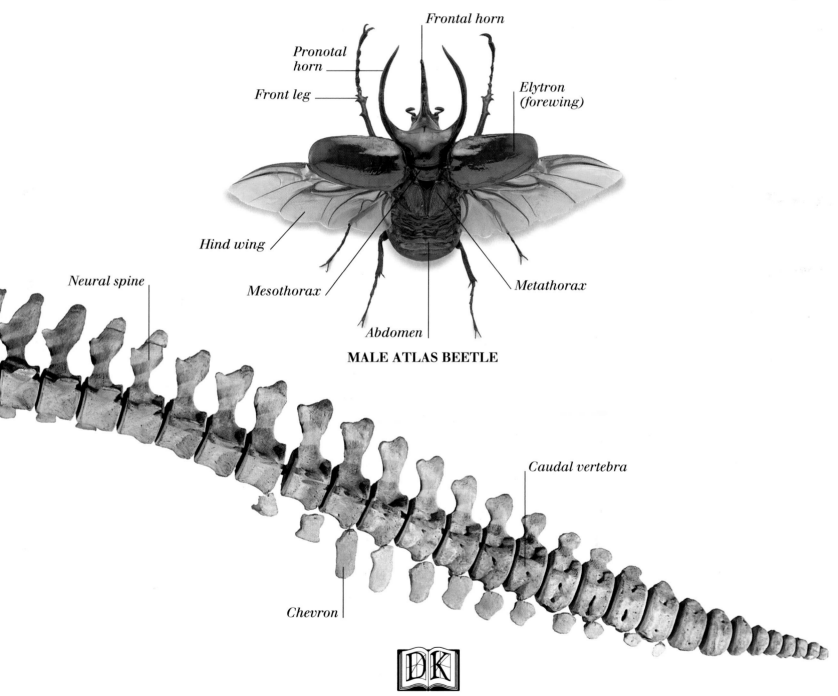

Frontal horn

Pronotal
horn

Front leg

Elytron
(forewing)

Hind wing

Neural spine

Mesothorax

Metathorax

Abdomen

MALE ATLAS BEETLE

Caudal vertebra

Chevron

DK

DORLING KINDERSLEY
LONDON • NEW YORK • STUTTGART

A DORLING KINDERSLEY BOOK

PROJECT ART EDITOR CHRIS WALKER
DESIGNER HELEN BENFIELD

PROJECT EDITOR FIONA COURTENAY-THOMPSON
EDITORIAL ASSISTANT WILL HODGKINSON
CONSULTANT EDITOR DR RICHARD WALKER

MANAGING ART EDITOR BRYN WALLS
MANAGING EDITORS RUTH MIDGLEY, MARTYN PAGE

ILLUSTRATIONS JOANNA CAMERON, DEBORAH MAIZELS, GRAHAM ROSEWARNE, JOHN TEMPERTON

PICTURE RESEARCH INGRID NILSSON

PRODUCTION HILARY STEPHENS

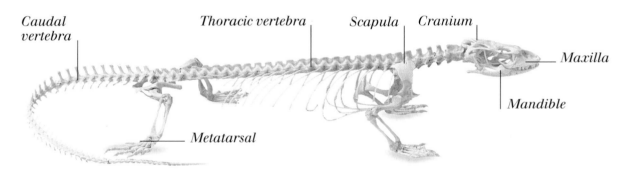

Caudal vertebra   *Thoracic vertebra*   *Scapula*   *Cranium*   *Maxilla*   *Mandible*   *Metatarsal*

MONITOR LIZARD SKELETON

FIRST PUBLISHED IN GREAT BRITAIN IN 1995
BY DORLING KINDERSLEY LIMITED
9 HENRIETTA STREET, LONDON WC2E 8PS

COPYRIGHT © 1995 DORLING KINDERSLEY LIMITED, LONDON

A CIP CATALOGUE RECORD FOR THIS BOOK IS AVAILABLE FROM THE BRITISH LIBRARY

ISBN 0 7513 1060 3

REPRODUCED BY COLOURSCAN, SINGAPORE
PRINTED AND BOUND BY ARNOLDO MONDADORI, VERONA, ITALY

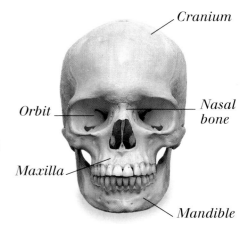

Cranium

Orbit

Nasal bone

Maxilla

Mandible

HUMAN SKULL

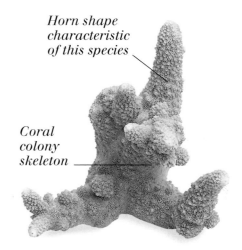

Horn shape characteristic of this species

Coral colony skeleton

CORAL COLONY SKELETON

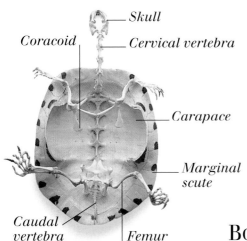

Prominent supraorbital ridge

Sloping forehead

Orbit

Deep, flat cheek-bone

HOMO ERECTUS SKULL

Contents

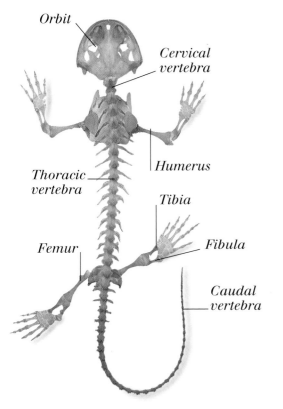

Skull

Coracoid

Cervical vertebra

Carapace

Marginal scute

Caudal vertebra

Femur

TURTLE SKELETON

Orbit

Cervical vertebra

Thoracic vertebra

Humerus

Femur

Tibia

Fibula

Caudal vertebra

SALAMANDER SKELETON

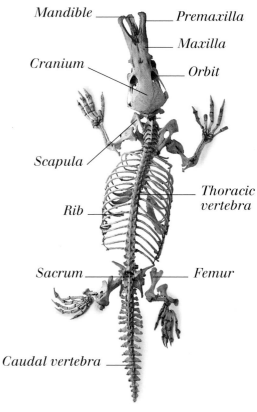

Mandible

Premaxilla

Maxilla

Cranium

Orbit

Scapula

Rib

Thoracic vertebra

Sacrum

Femur

Caudal vertebra

PLATYPUS SKELETON

Skeleton varieties 1

THE SKELETON IS A SUPPORTIVE framework
that maintains the shape of an organism and
protects its internal organs. In many animals,
the skeleton also plays a vital role in movement.
There are two main types of skeleton: internal
skeletons (endoskeletons) and external skeletons
(exoskeletons). Vertebrates (animals with backbones)
– fish, amphibians, reptiles, birds, and mammals –
have endoskeletons, which are usually made of bone.
A few vertebrates, such as boxfish and tortoises,
have both endoskeletons and exoskeletons.
Most invertebrates (animals without backbones)
have exoskeletons. These include the body cases
of insects and crustaceans, the shells of snails,
and the tests of sea urchins. Some single-celled
organisms also have exoskeletons; for example,
the outer coat of diatoms. Other types of skeleton
include the hydrostatic (fluid-filled) skeleton
of earthworms, and plant skeletons, which
consist of various elements, such as xylem,
that help to support roots, stems, and leaves.

PARROT SKELETON

Orbit
Upper mandible
Cranium
Auditory meatus
Cervical vertebra
Beak
Humerus
Femur
Radius
Ulna
Pygostyle
Lower mandible
Pelvis
Metacarpal
Coracoid
Furcula
Digit
Sternum
Rib
Keel of sternum
Tibiotarsus
Claw
Phalanx
Tarsometatarsus

FROG SKELETON

Suprascapula
Cranium
Frontoparietal bone
Lumbar vertebra
Nasal bone
Sacral vertebra
Maxilla
Mandible
Scapula
Femur
Sternum
Humerus
Pelvis
Radio-ulna
Carpal
Tibiofibula
Metacarpal
Calcaneus
Astragalus
Metatarsal
Phalanx

LIZARD SKELETON

Metacarpal
Cranium
Phalanx
Orbit
Cervical vertebra
Carpal
Radius
Scapula
Ulna
Rib
Thoracolumbar vertebra
Sacrum
Femur
Pelvis
Tibia
Tarsal
Phalanx
Metatarsal
Caudal vertebra

CARP SKELETON

Dorsal fin
Parietal bone
Neural spine
Vertebra
Frontal bone
Orbit
Femur
Caudal fin
Dentary bone
Haemal spine
Rib
Pectoral fin
Maxilla
Anal fin
Interhaemal
Pelvic fin
Opercular bone

BADGER SKELETON

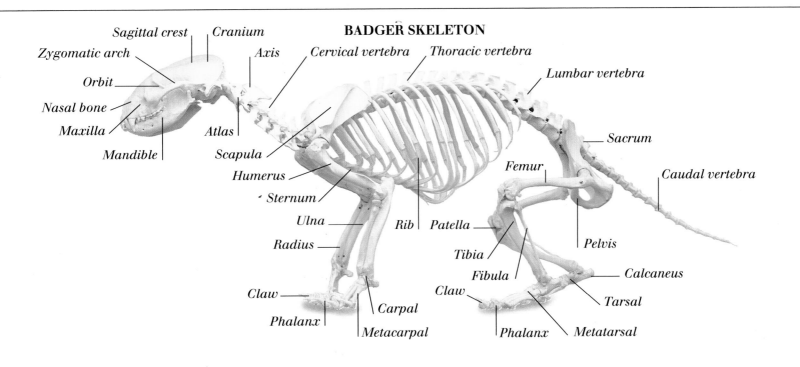

Sagittal crest
Cranium
Zygomatic arch
Axis
Cervical vertebra
Thoracic vertebra
Orbit
Lumbar vertebra
Nasal bone
Maxilla
Atlas
Mandible
Scapula
Humerus
Sacrum
Sternum
Femur
Caudal vertebra
Ulna
Rib
Patella
Radius
Tibia
Pelvis
Fibula
Calcaneus
Claw
Claw
Tarsal
Phalanx
Carpal
Metatarsal
Metacarpal
Phalanx

HUMAN SKELETON

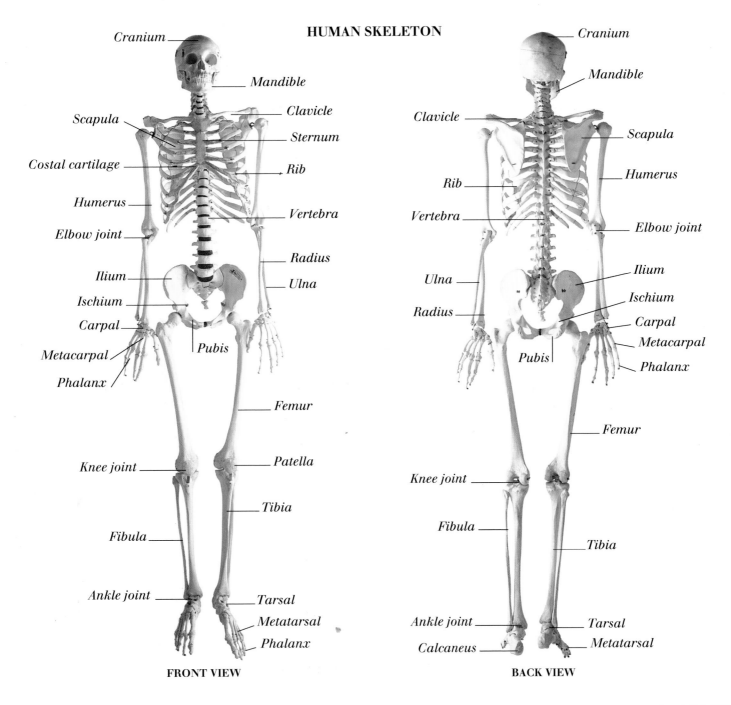

Cranium
Cranium
Mandible
Mandible
Clavicle
Scapula
Clavicle
Scapula
Sternum
Costal cartilage
Rib
Humerus
Humerus
Rib
Vertebra
Elbow joint
Vertebra
Elbow joint
Radius
Ilium
Ulna
Ilium
Ischium
Ischium
Carpal
Ulna
Carpal
Metacarpal
Radius
Metacarpal
Phalanx
Pubis
Phalanx
Pubis
Femur
Femur
Patella
Knee joint
Knee joint
Tibia
Fibula
Fibula
Tibia
Ankle joint
Tarsal
Ankle joint
Tarsal
Metatarsal
Metatarsal
Calcaneus
Phalanx

FRONT VIEW

BACK VIEW

Skeleton varieties 2

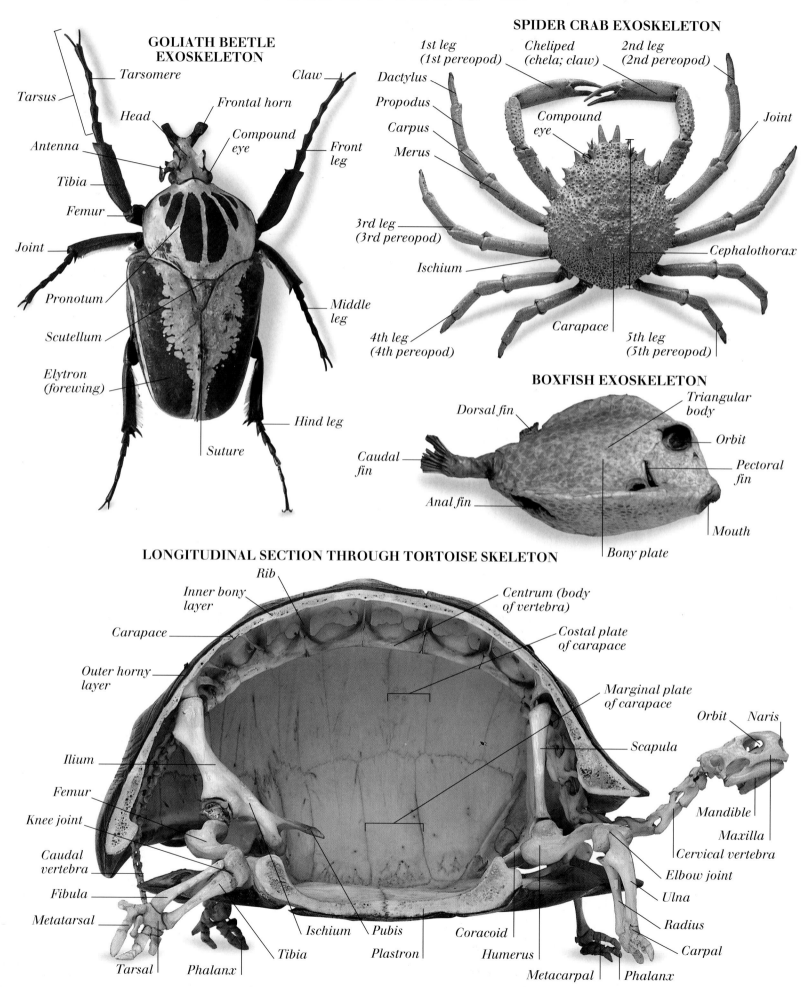

GOLIATH BEETLE EXOSKELETON

Tarsomere
Tarsus
Claw
Head
Frontal horn
Antenna
Compound eye
Front leg
Tibia
Femur
Joint
Pronotum
Scutellum
Middle leg
Elytron (forewing)
Hind leg
Suture

SPIDER CRAB EXOSKELETON

1st leg (1st pereopod)
Cheliped (chela; claw)
2nd leg (2nd pereopod)
Dactylus
Propodus
Compound eye
Joint
Carpus
Merus
3rd leg (3rd pereopod)
Cephalothorax
Ischium
Carapace
4th leg (4th pereopod)
5th leg (5th pereopod)

BOXFISH EXOSKELETON

Triangular body
Dorsal fin
Orbit
Caudal fin
Pectoral fin
Anal fin
Mouth
Bony plate

LONGITUDINAL SECTION THROUGH TORTOISE SKELETON

Rib
Inner bony layer
Centrum (body of vertebra)
Carapace
Costal plate of carapace
Outer horny layer
Marginal plate of carapace
Orbit
Naris
Scapula
Ilium
Femur
Mandible
Knee joint
Maxilla
Caudal vertebra
Cervical vertebra
Fibula
Elbow joint
Metatarsal
Ulna
Radius
Ischium
Pubis
Coracoid
Carpal
Tibia
Plastron
Humerus
Metacarpal
Phalanx
Tarsal
Phalanx

SEA URCHIN EXOSKELETON

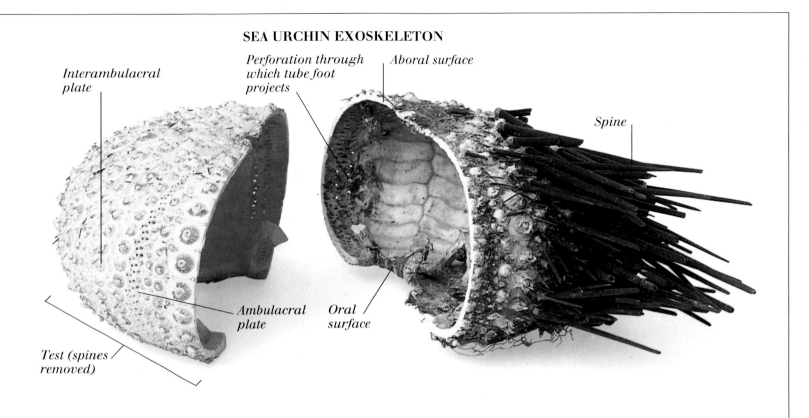

Interambulacral plate

Perforation through which tube foot projects

Aboral surface

Spine

Ambulacral plate

Oral surface

Test (spines removed)

DIATOM FRUSTULES

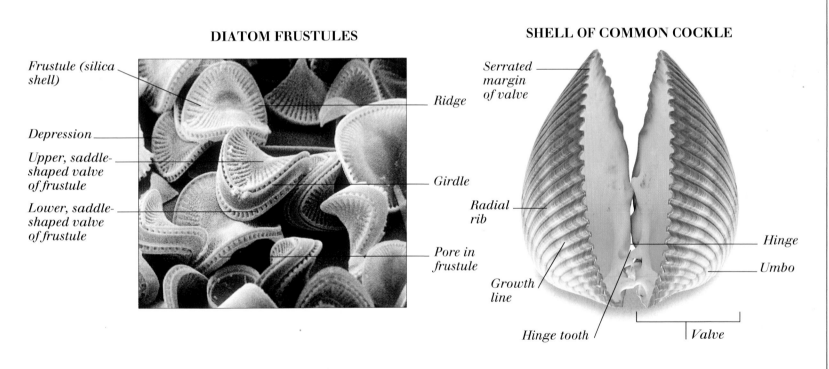

Frustule (silica shell)

Depression

Upper, saddle-shaped valve of frustule

Lower, saddle-shaped valve of frustule

Ridge

Girdle

Pore in frustule

SHELL OF COMMON COCKLE

Serrated margin of valve

Radial rib

Growth line

Hinge tooth

Hinge

Umbo

Valve

WORM HYDROSTATIC SKELETON

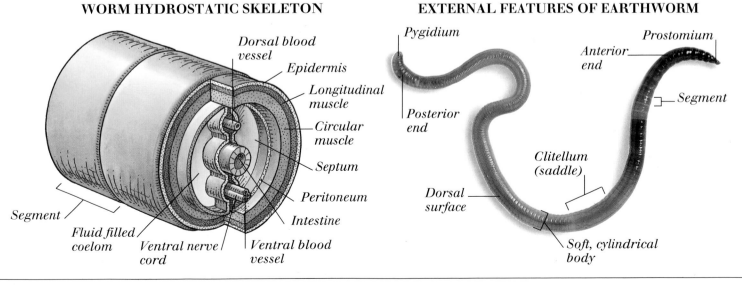

Dorsal blood vessel

Epidermis

Longitudinal muscle

Circular muscle

Septum

Peritoneum

Intestine

Ventral blood vessel

Segment

Fluid filled coelom

Ventral nerve cord

EXTERNAL FEATURES OF EARTHWORM

Pygidium

Prostomium

Anterior end

Segment

Posterior end

Clitellum (saddle)

Dorsal surface

Soft, cylindrical body

The human skelen through life

THE SKELETON OF THE HUMAN FETUS is formed from tough but flexible cartilage that acts as a blueprint for bone construction. During ossification (changing to bone), which begins before birth, the cartilage is broken down and the resulting space is filled by bone-building mineral salts and protein fibres secreted by bone cells. At birth, the diaphyses (shafts) of the long bones are already ossified, while the epiphyses (ends of bones) are still cartilaginous. The epiphyses gradually ossify, leaving a cartilaginous epiphyseal plate (growth plate) where growth continues until late adolescence. The bones of the skull are formed by the ossification of fibrous tissue, rather than cartilage. In the newborn baby, this flexible tissue forms fontanelles between the partly ossified skull bones, allowing the cranium to enlarge as the brain grows. The facial bones also enlarge as the skull develops. After the age of about 40, bone mass starts to decrease, a process that is sometimes accelerated by osteoporosis.

GROWTH OF HUMAN SKULL

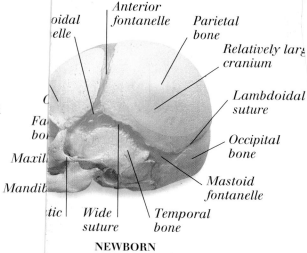

Anterior fontanelle
Parietal bone
Relatively larg cranium
oidal elle
Lambdoidal suture
Fa bo
Occipital bone
Maxill
Mandib
Mastoid fontanelle
tic
Wide suture
Temporal bone

NEWBORN

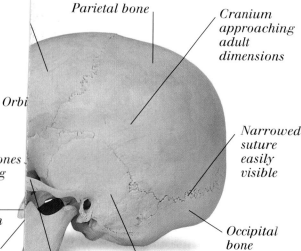

Parietal bone
Cranium approaching adult dimensions
Orbi
Narrowed suture easily visible
Facial bones enlarging
Deciduous (milk) tooth
Erupting permanent tooth
Occipital bone
Temporal bone
Zygomatic arch
Mandibulla

6 YEARS

PRIMARY OSSIFICATION CENTRES IN 12-WEEK-OLD FETUS

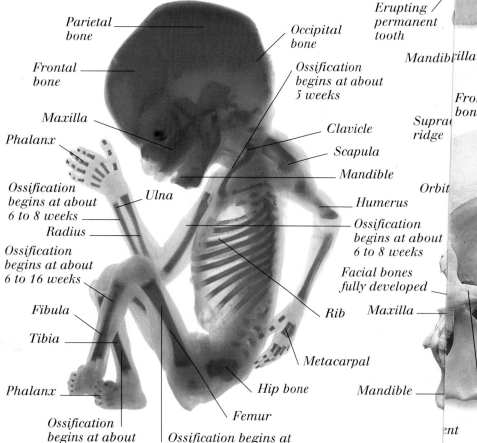

Parietal bone
Occipital bone
Frontal bone
Ossification begins at about 5 weeks
Maxilla
Clavicle
Phalanx
Scapula
Mandible
Ossification begins at about 6 to 8 weeks
Ulna
Humerus
Radius
Ossification begins at about 6 to 8 weeks
Ossification begins at about 6 to 16 weeks
Facial bones fully developed
Fibula
Maxilla
Rib
Tibia
Phalanx
Metacarpal
Hip bone
Femur
Ossification begins at about 6 to 12 weeks
Ossification begins at about 6 to 12 weeks

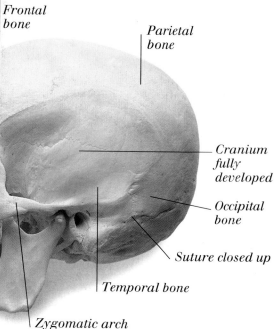

Frontal bone
Suprac ridge
Parietal bone
Orbit
Cranium fully developed
Facial bones fully developed
Occipital bone
Maxilla
Suture closed up
Mandible
Temporal bone
Zygomatic arch
ent

ADULT

rpals
er nter
ate
um

BONE DEVELOPMENT IN HUMAN HAND

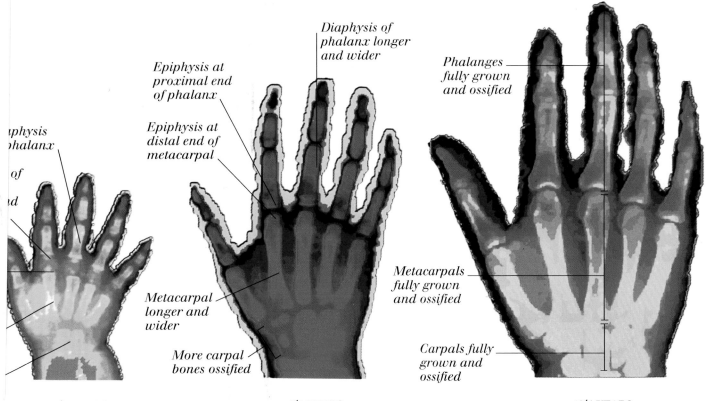

Diaphysis of phalanx longer and wider

Epiphysis at proximal end of phalanx

Epiphysis at distal end of metacarpal

Phalanges fully grown and ossified

iaphysis phalanx

of

nd

Metacarpal longer and wider

More carpal bones ossified

Metacarpals fully grown and ossified

Carpals fully grown and ossified

2½ YEARS

6½ YEARS

19½ YEARS

SCANNING ELECTRON MICROGRAPH OF CANCELLOUS BONE

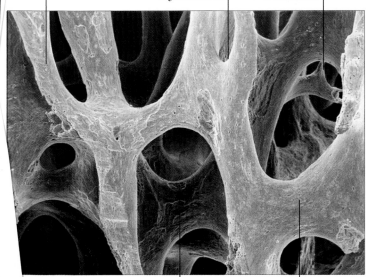

Trabecula

Trabecular bifurcation

Thin trabecula

Fewer trabeculae

Marrow space between trabeculae

Thick trabecula

Marrow space between trabeculae enlarged

Porous surface of trabecula weakened by loss of bone

HEALTHY BONE

BONE WITH OSTEOPOROSIS

Plant skeletons

SKELETON OF MAGNOLIA LEAF

PLANTS TYPICALLY HAVE A STEM that bears leaves and flowers, and roots that anchor the plant in the soil. The stem and roots are supported and protected by a skeletal system. The skeleton of the stem helps the plant to resist bending caused by external forces; it also holds the leaves in position so that they can receive the sunlight necessary for photosynthesis. The stems of herbaceous (non-woody) plants are supported by cells called sclerenchyma and collenchyma, and by strong-walled, water-conducting cells called xylem. In woody plants, the trunks and branches are supported by an inner core of xylem and associated fibres, which together form the wood. As the wood in the centre of the tree gets older, it loses its conductive role but continues to support the stem. This non-conducting wood is known as heartwood. The outer, conducting wood is known as sapwood. Roots have a central cylinder of transport tissue, known as the stele. The stele contains tough xylem that enables roots to resist the pressure produced as they grow through the soil.

MICROGRAPH OF XYLEM IN BUTTERCUP STEM

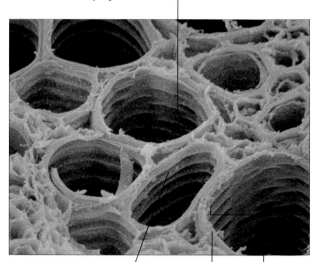

Lumen of xylem vessel

Annular thickening in wall of xylem vessel

Lignified cell wall of xylem vessel

Xylem vessel

LONGITUDINAL SECTION THROUGH BUTTERCUP ROOT

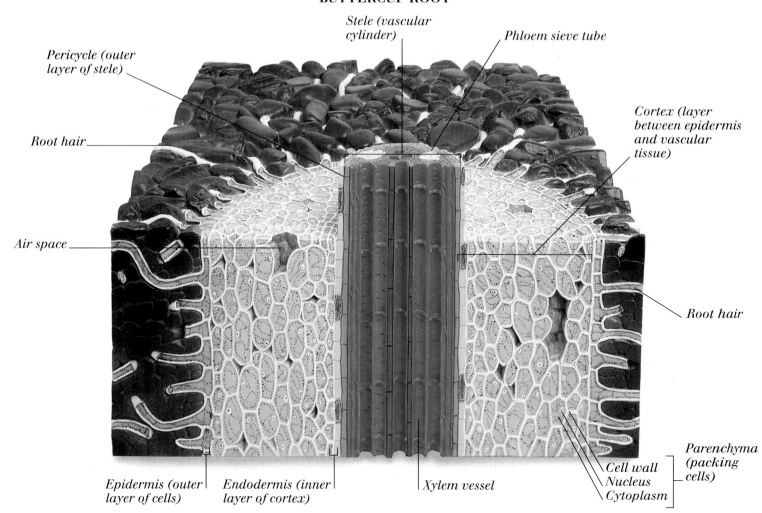

Stele (vascular cylinder)

Phloem sieve tube

Pericycle (outer layer of stele)

Cortex (layer between epidermis and vascular tissue)

Root hair

Air space

Root hair

Epidermis (outer layer of cells)

Endodermis (inner layer of cortex)

Xylem vessel

Cell wall
Nucleus
Cytoplasm

Parenchyma (packing cells)

TREE SHOWING EXTERNAL STRESSES

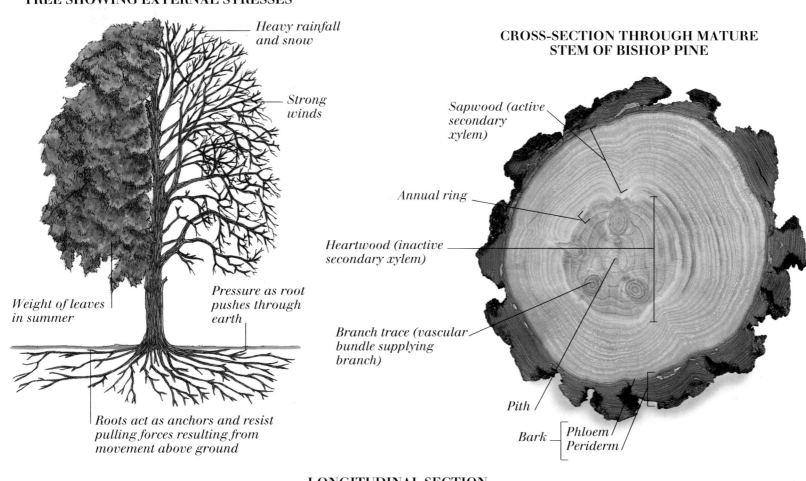

Heavy rainfall and snow

Strong winds

Weight of leaves in summer

Pressure as root pushes through earth

Roots act as anchors and resist pulling forces resulting from movement above ground

CROSS-SECTION THROUGH MATURE STEM OF BISHOP PINE

Sapwood (active secondary xylem)

Annual ring

Heartwood (inactive secondary xylem)

Branch trace (vascular bundle supplying branch)

Pith

Bark
Phloem
Periderm

LONGITUDINAL SECTION THROUGH YOUNG WOODY STEM

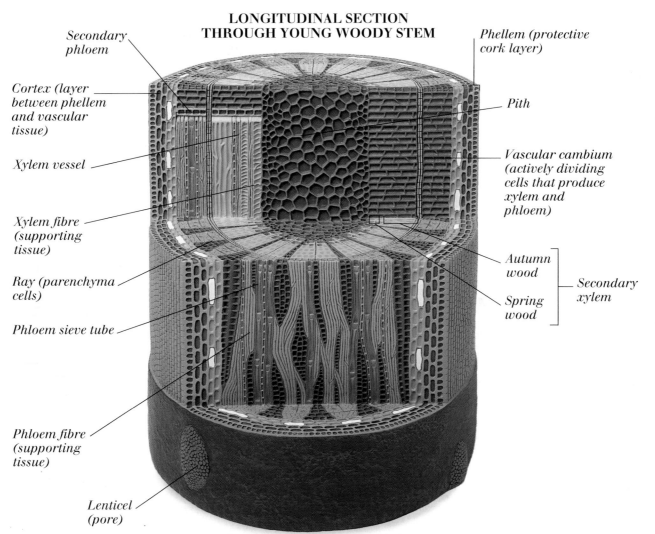

Secondary phloem

Cortex (layer between phellem and vascular tissue)

Xylem vessel

Xylem fibre (supporting tissue)

Ray (parenchyma cells)

Phloem sieve tube

Phloem fibre (supporting tissue)

Lenticel (pore)

Phellem (protective cork layer)

Pith

Vascular cambium (actively dividing cells that produce xylem and phloem)

Autumn wood

Spring wood

Secondary xylem

Shells and simple skeletons

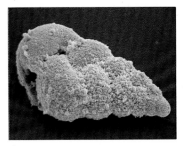

FOSSIL FORAMINIFERAN

SHELLS ARE EXOSKELETONS that protect the soft bodies of most molluscs. Each mollusc group has a characteristic shell form. Gastropods, such as the lightning whelk, have a cone-shaped, spiral shell, made up of tubular whorls, with an aperture through which the animal's head is extended or retracted. Bivalves, such as the mussel, have a hinged shell with two halves, that are opened and closed by powerful muscles. Cephalopods, such as the octopus, generally lack external shells. However, one cephalopod, *Nautilus*, has a flat-spiral shell, divided into chambers. *Nautilus* occupies only the body chamber. Some invertebrates have simple exoskeletons. Corals, for example, are colonial invertebrates that build protective calcium carbonate cases into which they can retreat. Foraminiferans are aquatic protozoans with a shell that protects their amoeboid body.

EXTERNAL FEATURES OF NAUTILUS

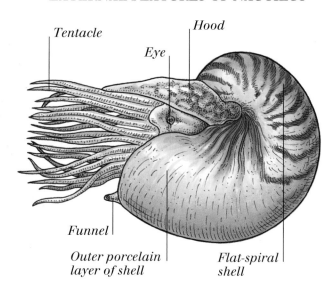

Tentacle

Eye

Hood

Funnel

Outer porcelain layer of shell

Flat-spiral shell

SECTION THROUGH NAUTILUS SHELL

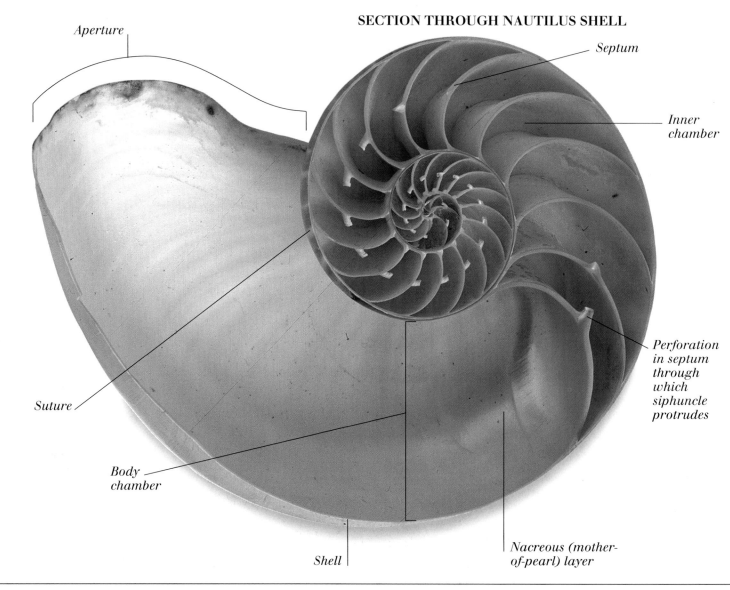

Aperture

Septum

Inner chamber

Perforation in septum through which siphuncle protrudes

Suture

Body chamber

Nacreous (mother-of-pearl) layer

Shell

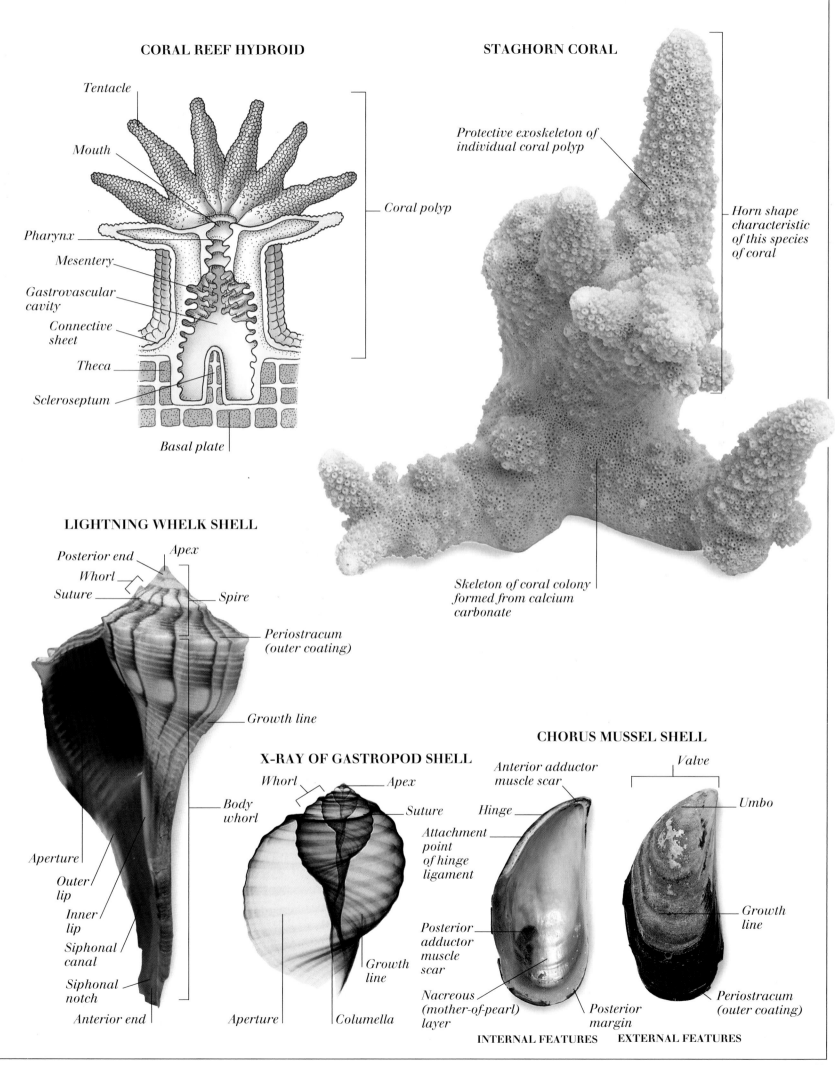

CORAL REEF HYDROID

Tentacle

Mouth

Pharynx

Mesentery

Gastrovascular
cavity

Connective
sheet

Theca

Scleroseptum

Basal plate

Coral polyp

STAGHORN CORAL

Protective exoskeleton of
individual coral polyp

Horn shape
characteristic
of this species
of coral

Skeleton of coral colony
formed from calcium
carbonate

LIGHTNING WHELK SHELL

Posterior end

Whorl

Suture

Apex

Spire

Periostracum
(outer coating)

Growth line

Body
whorl

Aperture

Outer
lip

Inner
lip

Siphonal
canal

Siphonal
notch

Anterior end

X-RAY OF GASTROPOD SHELL

Whorl

Apex

Suture

Growth
line

Aperture

Columella

CHORUS MUSSEL SHELL

Anterior adductor
muscle scar

Hinge

Attachment
point
of hinge
ligament

Posterior
adductor
muscle
scar

Nacreous
(mother-of-pearl)
layer

Posterior
margin

INTERNAL FEATURES

Valve

Umbo

Growth
line

Periostracum
(outer coating)

EXTERNAL FEATURES

Arthropod exoskeletons

TARANTULA MOULT

Most animals with exoskeletons belong to the arthropod group (animals with jointed limbs), which includes insects, such as beetles; arachnids, such as scorpions; and crustaceans, such as crabs. The arthropod exoskeleton, also known as the cuticle, encases the entire body (including the eyes), and consists of inflexible plates that meet at flexible joints. The joints are formed by thinner sections of cuticle called articular membranes. Muscles, attached to the exoskeleton across these joints, contract to produce movement. The arthropod exoskeleton cannot expand, and must be moulted periodically to allow the animal to grow. An exoskeleton also imposes a maximum size on arthropods: although the cuticle contains a substance called chitin that makes it both hard and light, above a certain body size the cuticle becomes so heavy that movement is impossible.

WALKING MECHANISM OF INSECT

Protractor muscle (pulls limb forwards)
Cuticle
Flexor muscle (pulls limb downwards)
Retractor muscle (pulls limb backwards)
Notum
Pleuron
Sternum
Limb
Joint
Extensor muscle (pulls limb upwards)

MECHANISM IN BODY

Extensor muscle (straightens joint)
Articular membrane
Condyle
Cuticle
Flexor muscle bends joint

MECHANISM IN LEG

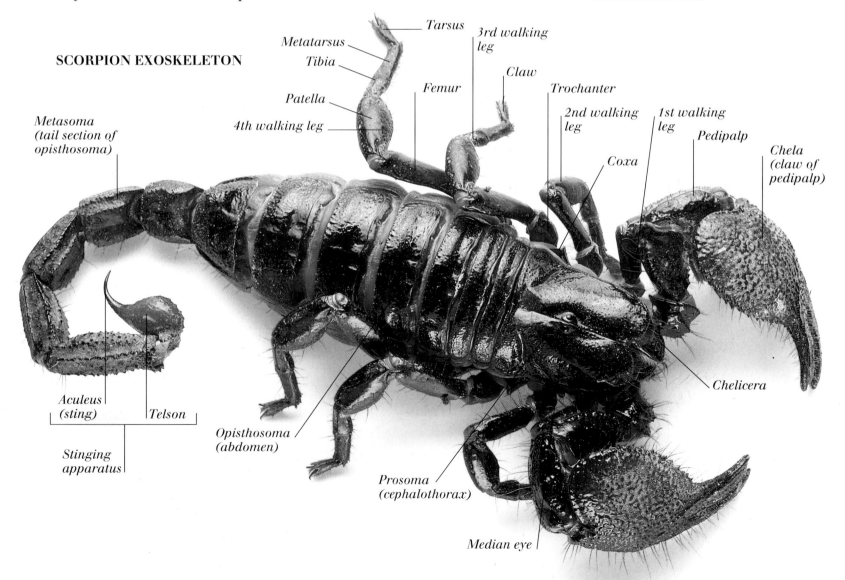

SCORPION EXOSKELETON

Tarsus
Metatarsus
3rd walking leg
Tibia
Claw
Femur
Trochanter
Patella
2nd walking leg
1st walking leg
4th walking leg
Pedipalp
Metasoma (tail section of opisthosoma)
Coxa
Chela (claw of pedipalp)
Chelicera
Aculeus (sting)
Telson
Opisthosoma (abdomen)
Stinging apparatus
Prosoma (cephalothorax)
Median eye

CRAB EXOSKELETON

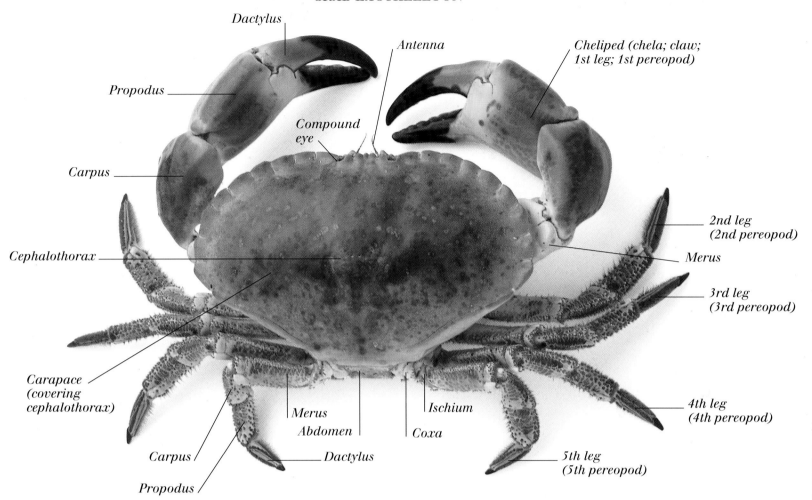

Dactylus

Antenna

Cheliped (chela; claw; 1st leg; 1st pereopod)

Propodus

Compound eye

Carpus

2nd leg (2nd pereopod)

Merus

Cephalothorax

3rd leg (3rd pereopod)

Carapace (covering cephalothorax)

Merus

Abdomen

Ischium

Coxa

4th leg (4th pereopod)

Carpus

Dactylus

Propodus

5th leg (5th pereopod)

FLYING MECHANISM OF INSECT

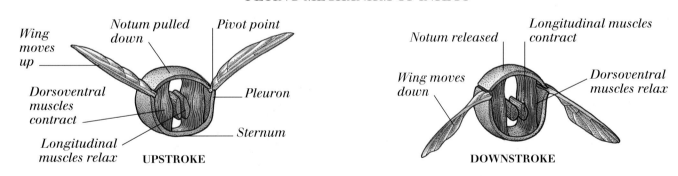

Wing moves up

Notum pulled down

Pivot point

Dorsoventral muscles contract

Pleuron

Longitudinal muscles relax

Sternum

UPSTROKE

Notum released

Longitudinal muscles contract

Wing moves down

Dorsoventral muscles relax

DOWNSTROKE

EXOSKELETON OF MALE ATLAS BEETLE

CROSS-SECTION THROUGH CUTICLE

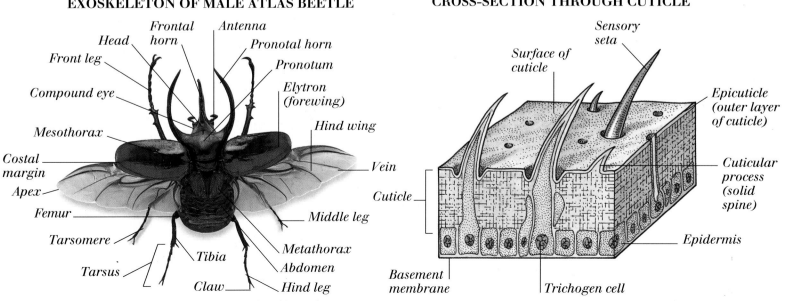

Frontal horn

Antenna

Head

Pronotal horn

Front leg

Pronotum

Compound eye

Elytron (forewing)

Mesothorax

Hind wing

Costal margin

Vein

Apex

Femur

Middle leg

Tarsomere

Tarsus

Tibia

Metathorax

Abdomen

Claw

Hind leg

Sensory seta

Surface of cuticle

Epicuticle (outer layer of cuticle)

Cuticle

Cuticular process (solid spine)

Epidermis

Basement membrane

Trichogen cell

Fish skeletons

FISHES WERE THE FIRST VERTEBRATES to evolve, and the first animals to have endoskeletons (internal skeletons). Bony fishes, such as cod and salmon, have a skeleton made of bone, as do most other vertebrates. Cartilaginous fishes, such as sharks (including dogfish) and rays, have a skeleton made of cartilage: a strong, flexible material that is also found in the human ear and nose. The fish skeleton produces a streamlined shape, adapting the animal for movement in water. It also has fins for propelling, stabilizing, and steering. The tapering skull minimizes drag as the fish moves forwards, and supports and protects the brain and gills. The flexible backbone (vertebral column) has muscles attached on either side along its length. These muscles contract alternately, bending the body from side to side to propel the fish forwards through the water. The fins, including the tail, are supported by bones and rods. The dorsal and ventral fins, positioned on the midline, prevent the fish from rolling; the paired pectoral and pelvic fins allow it to control its direction.

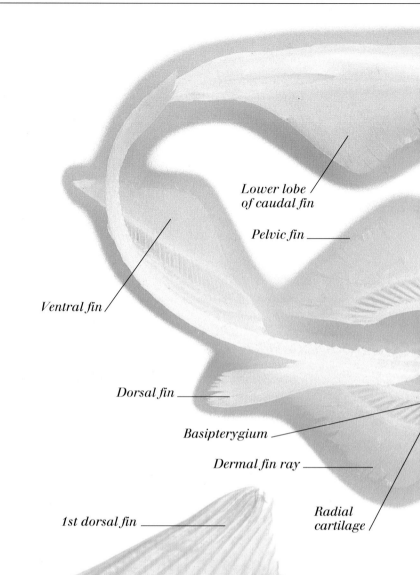

Lower lobe
of caudal fin

Pelvic fin

Ventral fin

Dorsal fin

Basipterygium

Dermal fin ray

1st dorsal fin

Radial
cartilage

COD SKELETON

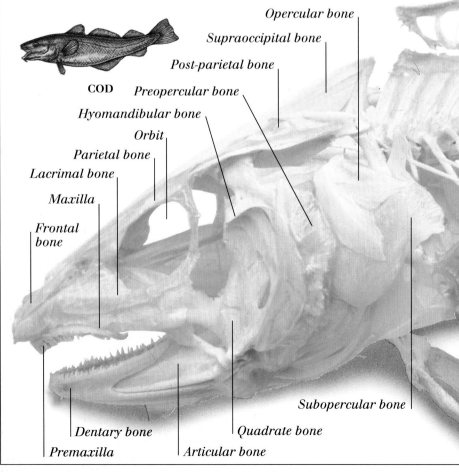

Opercular bone

Supraoccipital bone

Post-parietal bone

COD   Preopercular bone

Hyomandibular bone

Orbit

Parietal bone

Lacrimal bone

Maxilla

Frontal
bone

Rib

Pectoral fin

Dorsal process of
pectoral girdle

Subopercular bone

Pelvic fin

Dentary bone   Quadrate bone

Premaxilla   Articular bone

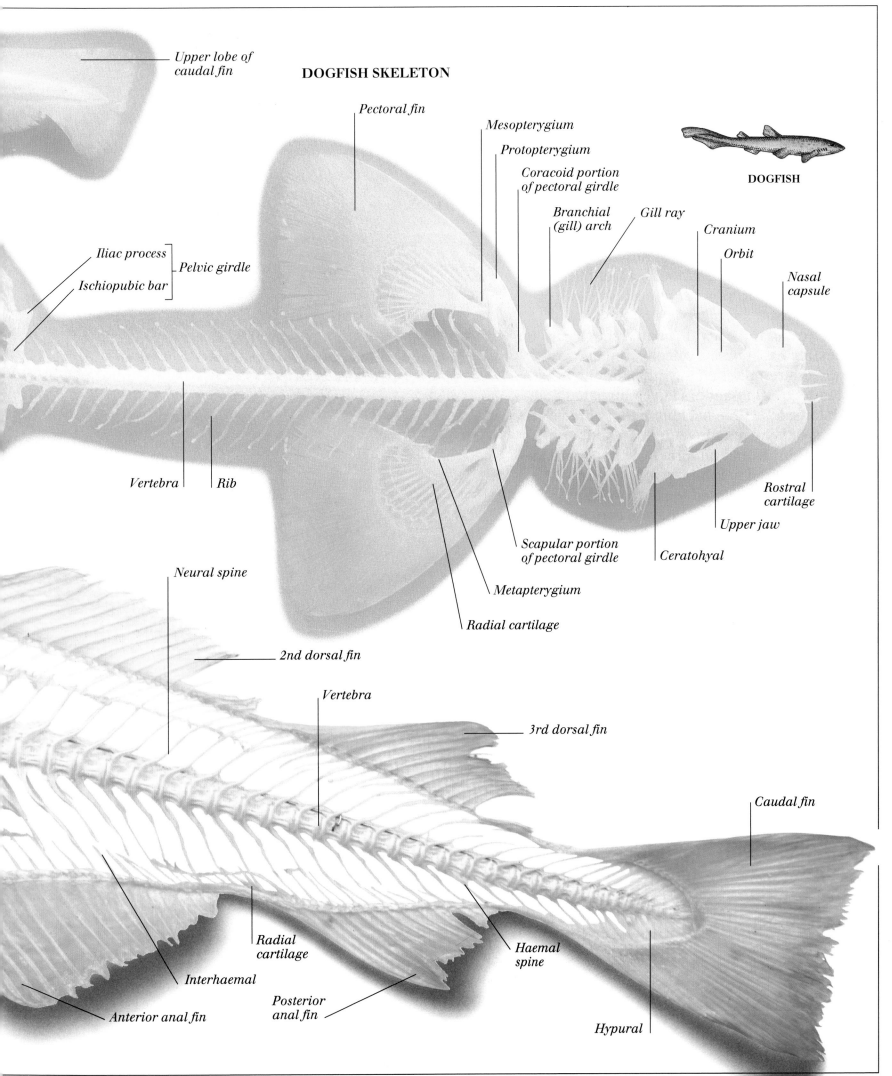

DOGFISH SKELETON

Upper lobe of
caudal fin

Pectoral fin

Mesopterygium

Protopterygium

Coracoid portion
of pectoral girdle

Branchial
(gill) arch

Gill ray

Cranium

Orbit

Nasal
capsule

DOGFISH

Iliac process

Ischiopubic bar

Pelvic girdle

Vertebra

Rib

Scapular portion
of pectoral girdle

Metapterygium

Radial cartilage

Rostral
cartilage

Upper jaw

Ceratohyal

Neural spine

2nd dorsal fin

Vertebra

3rd dorsal fin

Caudal fin

Radial
cartilage

Interhaemal

Anterior anal fin

Posterior
anal fin

Haemal
spine

Hypural

23

Reptile skeletons 1

REPTILES ARE VERTEBRATES with a bony endoskeleton. Typically, the reptile skeleton is elongated, with a flexible backbone and short legs that project sideways. However, skeletal variations occur within the group. For example, snakes lack limbs but have a long backbone consisting of between about 180 and 400 vertebrae. Snakes also have a highly flexible jaw mechanism, allowing large prey to be swallowed whole. Turtles have both an exoskeleton and an endoskeleton. The exoskeleton consists of a shell with an outer, horny layer and an inner, bony layer. The ribs, backbone, pectoral (shoulder) and pelvic (hip) girdles of the endoskeleton are fused to the inner layer of the exoskeleton. Crocodilians, such as the gharial and the Nile crocodile, are semi-aquatic reptiles with a long tail for swimming; a long snout with pointed teeth, and nostrils and eye sockets set high on the skull. Lizards generally follow the typical reptile body plan, but many also have features adapted to their environment, such as the tree-dwelling chameleon, which has opposable toes and a prehensile tail for grasping branches. Lizard-like tuataras retain primitive reptilian features, such as two complete temporal fenestrae (openings in the skull) and teeth that are fused to the jaw.

SNAKE SKELETON

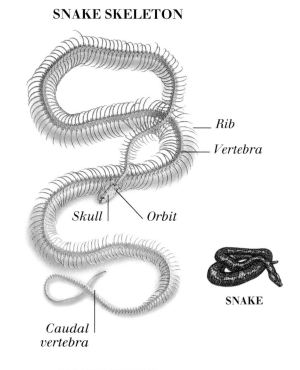

Rib
Vertebra
Skull
Orbit
Caudal vertebra

SNAKE

GHARIAL SKULL

Articular bone
Squamosal bone
Quadrate bone
Parietal bone
Infratemporal fenestra
Frontal bone
Postorbital bone
Orbit
Jugal bone
Maxilla
Premaxilla
Surangular bone
Angular bone
Mandibular fenestra
Dentary bone
Mandible
Naris

SNAKE SKULL

Orbit
Frontal bone
Premaxilla
Parietal bone
Maxilla
Supratemporal bone
Postfrontal bone
Quadrate bone
Ectopterygoid bone
Pterygoid bone
Articular bone
Surangular bone
Dentary bone

GHARIAL

Caudal vertebrae

Sacrum
Lumbar vertebrae
Rib

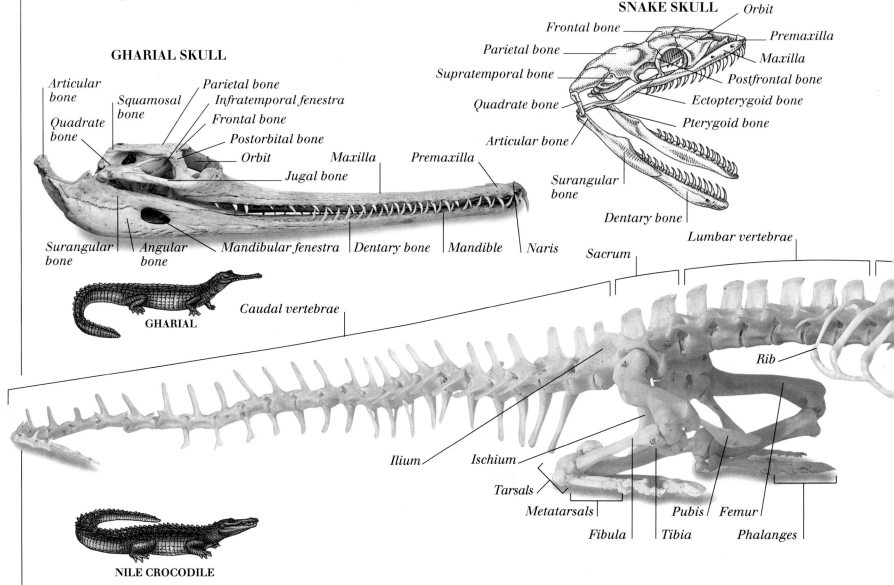

Ilium
Ischium
Tarsals
Metatarsals
Fibula
Tibia
Pubis
Femur
Phalanges

NILE CROCODILE

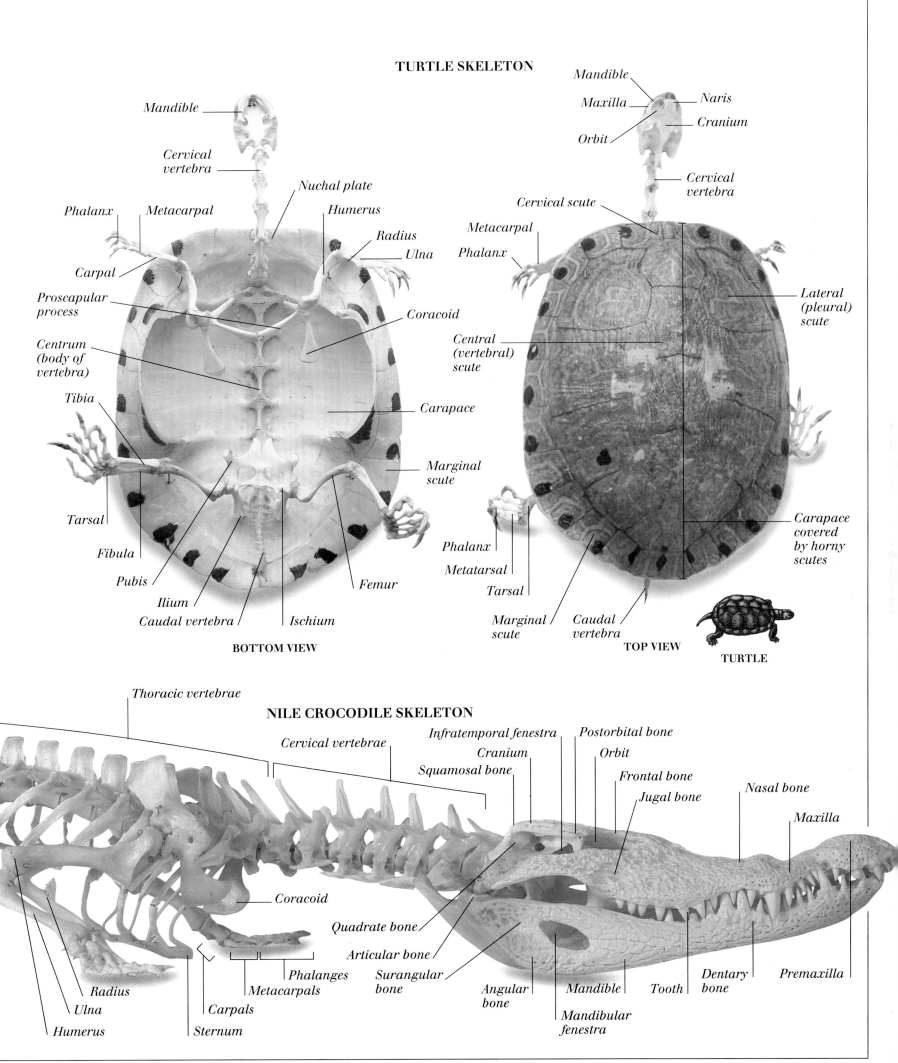

TURTLE SKELETON

Mandible

Cervical vertebra

Nuchal plate

Phalanx | **Metacarpal** | **Humerus**

Radius

Ulna

Carpal

Proscapular process

Coracoid

Centrum (body of vertebra)

Tibia

Carapace

Marginal scute

Tarsal

Fibula

Pubis

Ilium

Caudal vertebra

Ischium

Femur

BOTTOM VIEW

Mandible

Maxilla

Naris

Cranium

Orbit

Cervical vertebra

Cervical scute

Metacarpal

Phalanx

Lateral (pleural) scute

Central (vertebral) scute

Phalanx

Metatarsal

Tarsal

Marginal scute

Caudal vertebra

Carapace covered by horny scutes

TOP VIEW

TURTLE

NILE CROCODILE SKELETON

Thoracic vertebrae

Cervical vertebrae

Infratemporal fenestra

Cranium

Squamosal bone

Postorbital bone

Orbit

Frontal bone

Jugal bone

Nasal bone

Maxilla

Coracoid

Quadrate bone

Articular bone

Surangular bone

Angular bone

Mandible

Tooth

Dentary bone

Premaxilla

Mandibular fenestra

Radius

Ulna

Humerus

Phalanges

Metacarpals

Carpals

Sternum

Reptile skeletons 2

MONITOR LIZARD SKELETON

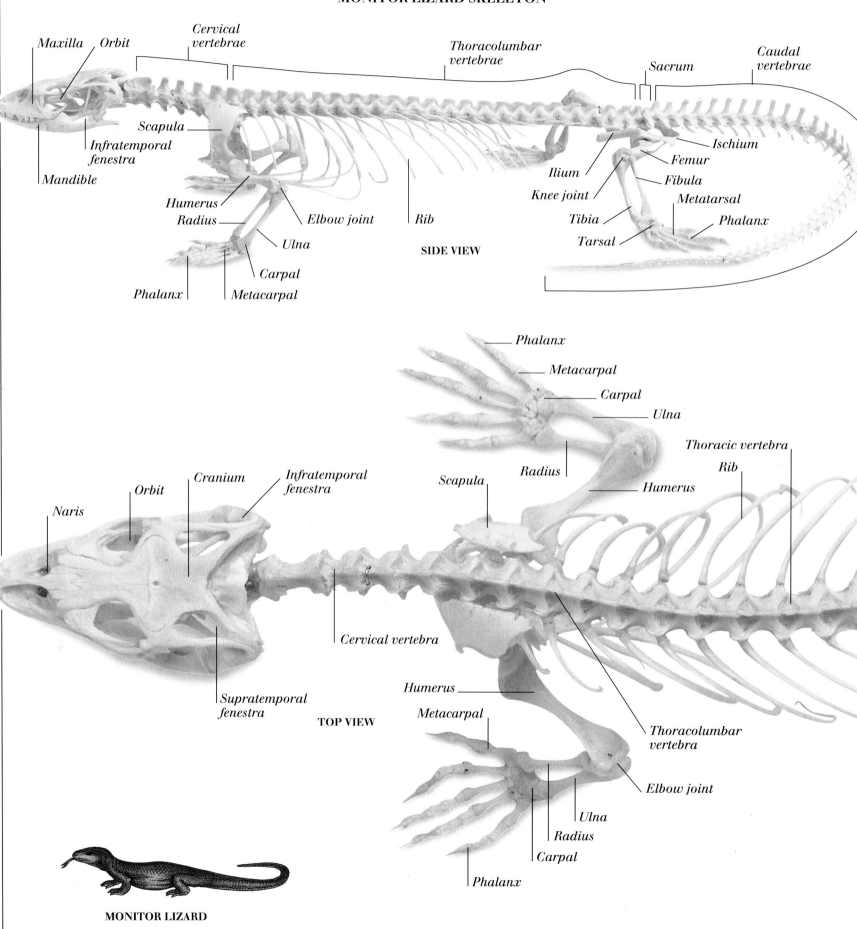

Maxilla   Orbit

Cervical vertebrae

Thoracolumbar vertebrae

Sacrum

Caudal vertebrae

Infratemporal fenestra

Mandible

Scapula

Ischium

Ilium

Femur

Fibula

Knee joint

Metatarsal

Humerus

Radius

Tibia

Phalanx

Ulna

Tarsal

Elbow joint

Rib

SIDE VIEW

Carpal

Phalanx   Metacarpal

Phalanx

Metacarpal

Carpal

Ulna

Naris

Orbit

Cranium

Infratemporal fenestra

Scapula

Radius

Thoracic vertebra

Rib

Humerus

Cervical vertebra

Supratemporal fenestra

Humerus

TOP VIEW

Metacarpal

Thoracolumbar vertebra

Elbow joint

Ulna

Radius

Carpal

Phalanx

MONITOR LIZARD

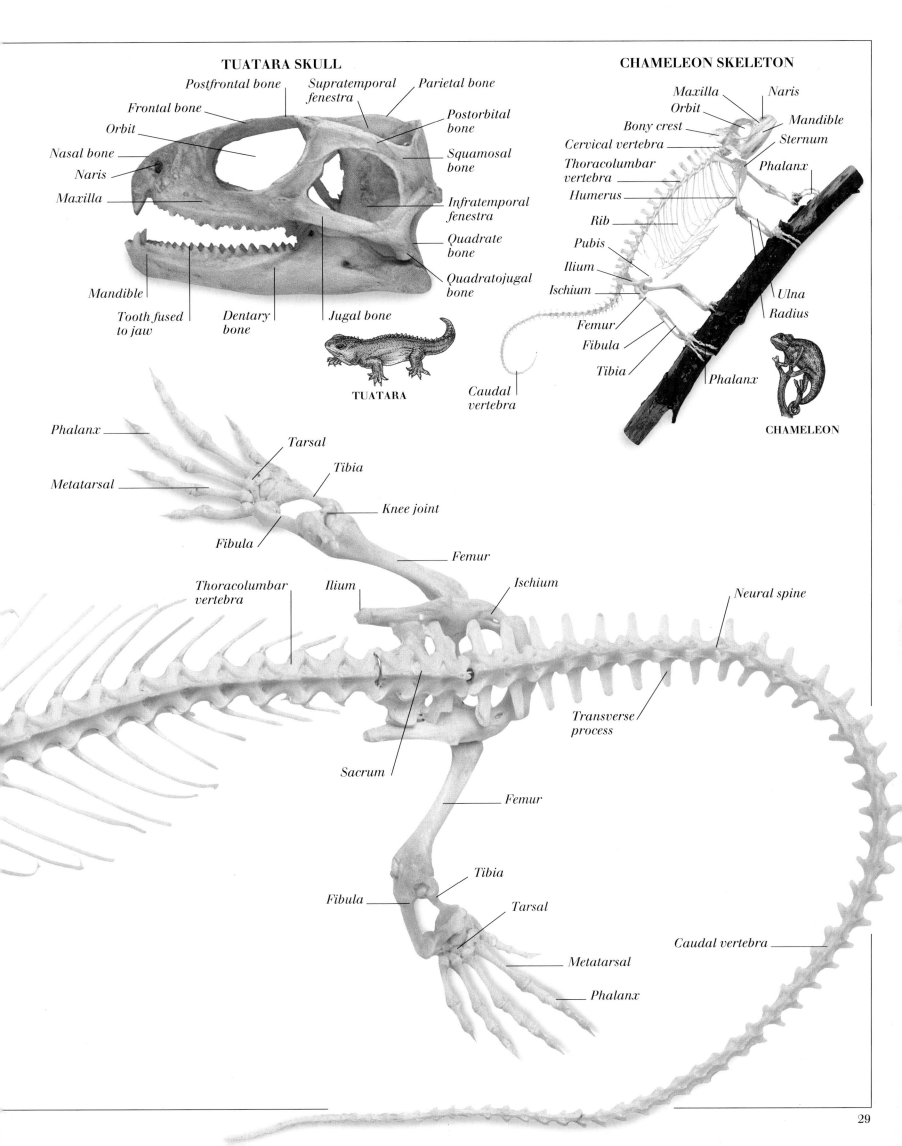

TUATARA SKULL

Postfrontal bone

Supratemporal fenestra

Parietal bone

Frontal bone

Postorbital bone

Orbit

Nasal bone

Squamosal bone

Naris

Maxilla

Infratemporal fenestra

Quadrate bone

Mandible

Quadratojugal bone

Tooth fused to jaw

Dentary bone

Jugal bone

TUATARA

Caudal vertebra

CHAMELEON SKELETON

Maxilla

Naris

Orbit

Mandible

Bony crest

Sternum

Cervical vertebra

Phalanx

Thoracolumbar vertebra

Humerus

Rib

Pubis

Ilium

Ischium

Ulna

Radius

Femur

Fibula

Tibia

Phalanx

CHAMELEON

Phalanx

Tarsal

Metatarsal

Tibia

Fibula

Knee joint

Femur

Thoracolumbar vertebra

Ilium

Ischium

Neural spine

Sacrum

Transverse process

Femur

Tibia

Fibula

Tarsal

Caudal vertebra

Metatarsal

Phalanx

Bird skeletons

MOST BIRDS HAVE SKELETONS ADAPTED for flight. The majority of these adaptations serve to make the skeleton lighter; they include hollow bones strengthened with struts; the fusing of some bones, such as the tarsometatarsus; a lightweight, horny beak instead of a heavy jawbone and teeth; forelimbs modified to form wings; and a sternum (breastbone) enlarged to form a central keel to which the powerful flight muscles – the pectoralis and supracoracoideus – are attached. The backbone (vertebral column) is also relatively short to increase stability during flight. Birds have resilient legs that provide support, enable them to walk, push the body off the ground at take-off, and absorb most of the force of landing. The skeletons of flightless birds show adaptations for different types of movement. For example, the penguin is well adapted for aquatic life by having forelimbs and hind limbs modified for swimming under water.

BONE STRUCTURE

Lightweight, honeycombed interior

Bifurcation

Supporting strut

Air-filled space

WING BONE

Dense, honeycombed interior

Supporting strut

Bifurcation

Air-filled space

SKULL BONE

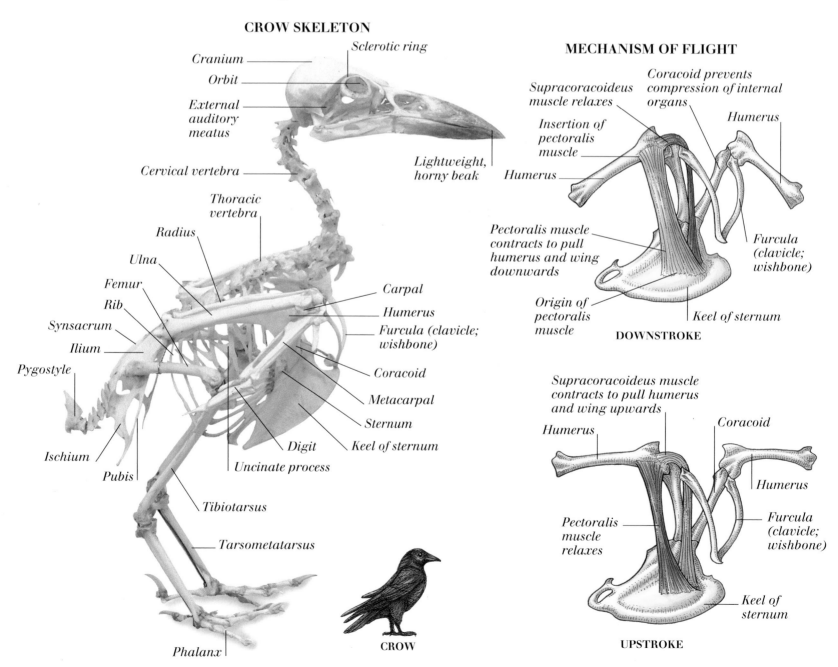

CROW SKELETON

Cranium

Orbit

External auditory meatus

Sclerotic ring

Lightweight, horny beak

Cervical vertebra

Thoracic vertebra

Radius

Ulna

Femur

Rib

Synsacrum

Ilium

Pygostyle

Ischium

Pubis

Tibiotarsus

Tarsometatarsus

Phalanx

Carpal

Humerus

Furcula (clavicle; wishbone)

Coracoid

Metacarpal

Sternum

Keel of sternum

Digit

Uncinate process

CROW

MECHANISM OF FLIGHT

Supracoracoideus muscle relaxes

Coracoid prevents compression of internal organs

Humerus

Insertion of pectoralis muscle

Humerus

Pectoralis muscle contracts to pull humerus and wing downwards

Furcula (clavicle; wishbone)

Origin of pectoralis muscle

Keel of sternum

DOWNSTROKE

Supracoracoideus muscle contracts to pull humerus and wing upwards

Humerus

Coracoid

Pectoralis muscle relaxes

Humerus

Furcula (clavicle; wishbone)

Keel of sternum

UPSTROKE

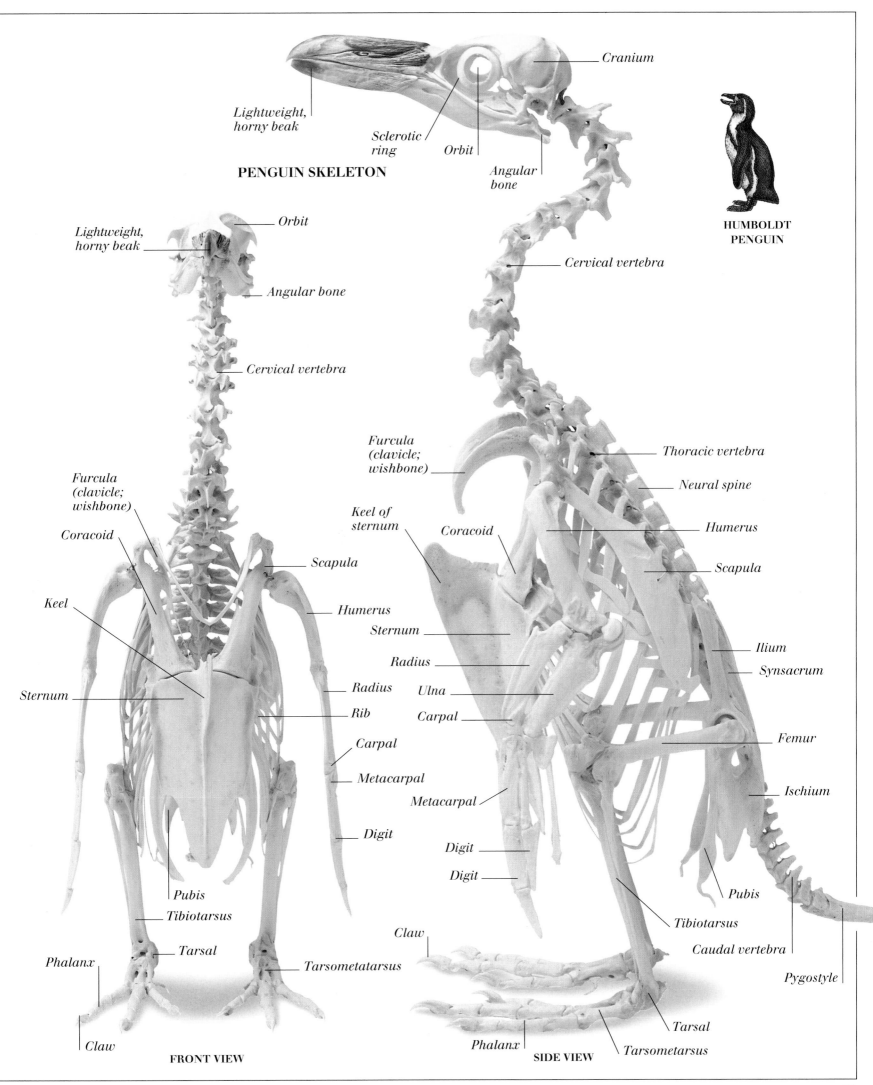

PENGUIN SKELETON

Lightweight, horny beak

Sclerotic ring

Orbit

Cranium

Angular bone

HUMBOLDT PENGUIN

Lightweight, horny beak

Orbit

Angular bone

Cervical vertebra

Cervical vertebra

Furcula (clavicle; wishbone)

Thoracic vertebra

Neural spine

Keel of sternum

Coracoid

Humerus

Coracoid

Scapula

Scapula

Keel

Humerus

Sternum

Sternum

Radius

Radius

Ilium

Rib

Ulna

Synsacrum

Carpal

Carpal

Metacarpal

Femur

Metacarpal

Digit

Ischium

Pubis

Digit

Digit

Tibiotarsus

Pubis

Claw

Tibiotarsus

Phalanx

Tarsal

Caudal vertebra

Claw

Tarsometatarsus

Phalanx

Tarsal

Tarsometarsus

Pygostyle

FRONT VIEW

SIDE VIEW

31

Sea mammal skeletons

SEA MAMMALS INCLUDE ANIMALS that spend their life in
water, such as whales and dolphins, and those that live
mostly in water but come ashore to breed, such as seals,
sea lions, and walruses. All evolved from land-living mammals,
and their skeletons show numerous adaptations to aquatic life.
Seal forelimbs and hind limbs are modified to form flippers,
with short arm and leg bones and long phalanges (finger and
toe bones). Earless seals use their front flippers for steering
and their hind flippers for propulsion. In contrast, fur seals
and sea lions use their front flippers for propulsion and their
hind flippers for steering. The backbone of seals is highly
flexible, allowing rapid turning in water and caterpillar-like
shuffling movements on land. The whale skeleton produces
a streamlined, fish-like shape, with an elongated head, a
short neck, and a long, tapering body with no hind limbs.
The forelimbs, which are used for steering, have shortened
arm bones and extra phalanges (finger bones) to increase
rigidity. Muscles attached above and below the whale's
long, flexible backbone contract alternately to move the
tail flukes up and down and produce forward thrust.

Lumbar
vertebrae

Sacrum

Caudal
vertebrae

Ilium

Ischium

Femur

Tibia

Fibula

Tarsals

Metatarsals

Lumbar vertebrae

Phalanges

SEAL

Caudal vertebrae

Transverse
process

Chevron

Neural spine

KILLER WHALE

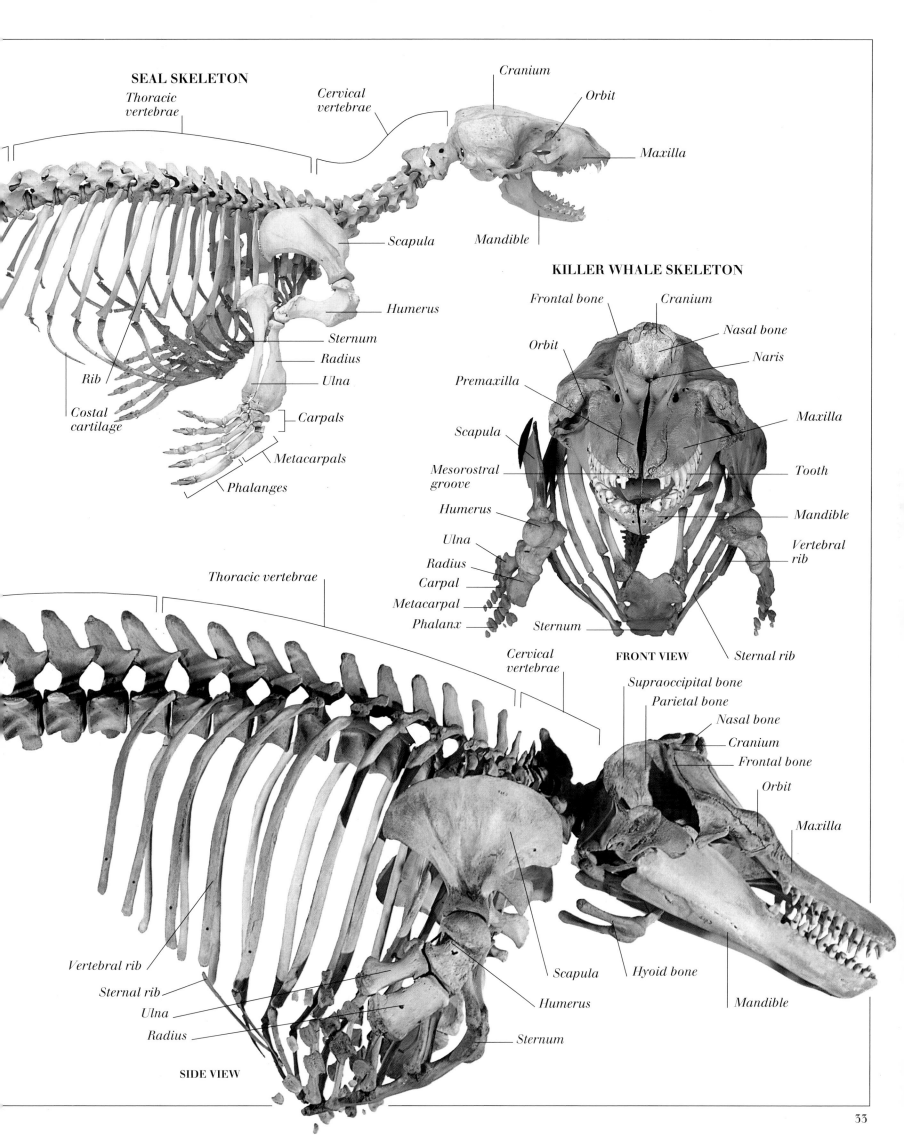

SEAL SKELETON

Thoracic vertebrae

Cervical vertebrae

Cranium

Orbit

Maxilla

Mandible

Scapula

Humerus

Sternum

Radius

Ulna

Rib

Costal cartilage

Carpals

Metacarpals

Phalanges

KILLER WHALE SKELETON

Frontal bone

Cranium

Orbit

Nasal bone

Premaxilla

Naris

Scapula

Maxilla

Mesorostral groove

Tooth

Humerus

Mandible

Ulna

Vertebral rib

Radius

Carpal

Metacarpal

Phalanx

Sternum

Sternal rib

Cervical vertebrae

FRONT VIEW

Thoracic vertebrae

Supraoccipital bone

Parietal bone

Nasal bone

Cranium

Frontal bone

Orbit

Maxilla

Vertebral rib

Scapula

Sternal rib

Humerus

Ulna

Hyoid bone

Radius

Sternum

Mandible

SIDE VIEW

33

Land mammal skeletons 1

LAND MAMMALS, unlike those that live in the sea, are not supported by the medium that surrounds them. Their entire weight is supported by the skeleton, in particular the strong backbone (vertebral column), and limbs that act as struts to hold the body off the ground. Mammals vary in the way the limbs support their body weight. In small, scampering mammals, such as squirrels and guinea pigs, the whole foot lies flat on the ground. Larger mammals typically raise the heel off the ground: cats and tigers walk on their toes; horses walk on one hoofed digit. The elephant has pillar-like limb bones to support its weight. However, not all land mammals fit into this pattern. For example, the platypus has short, broad limbs, but is adapted more for swimming than walking, whereas the bat's forelimbs are adapted for flight. The kangaroo hops on its hind limbs and uses its tail for balance and support.

BAT SKELETON

BAT

Skull

Carpal

Mandible

Clavicle

Sternum

Radius

Metacarpal

Thoracic vertebra

Femur

Ulna

Tibia

Tarsal

Phalanx

Metatarsal

Phalanx

PLATYPUS SKELETON

Premaxilla

Mandible

Maxilla

Cranium

Atlas

Claw

Orbit

Axis

Phalanx

Metacarpal

Scapula

Carpal

Radius

Ulna

Humerus

Rib

Costal enlargement of rib

Epipubic bone

Sacrum

Femur

Ilium

Ischium

Fibula

Phalanx

Tibia

Metatarsal

Tarsal

Patella

PLATYPUS

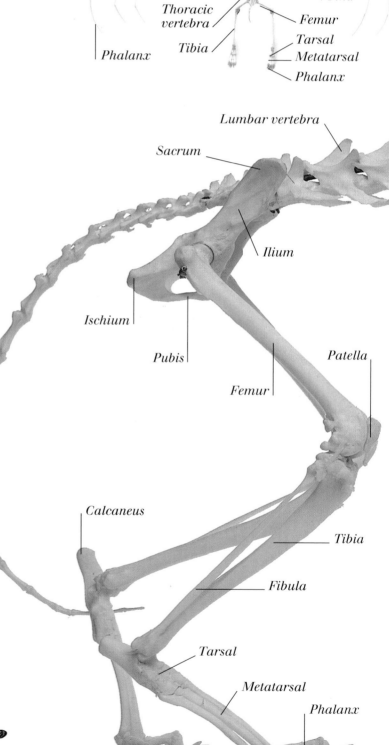

Lumbar vertebra

Sacrum

Ilium

Ischium

Caudal vertebra

Pubis

Patella

Femur

Calcaneus

Tibia

Fibula

Tarsal

Metatarsal

Phalanx

Retractable claw

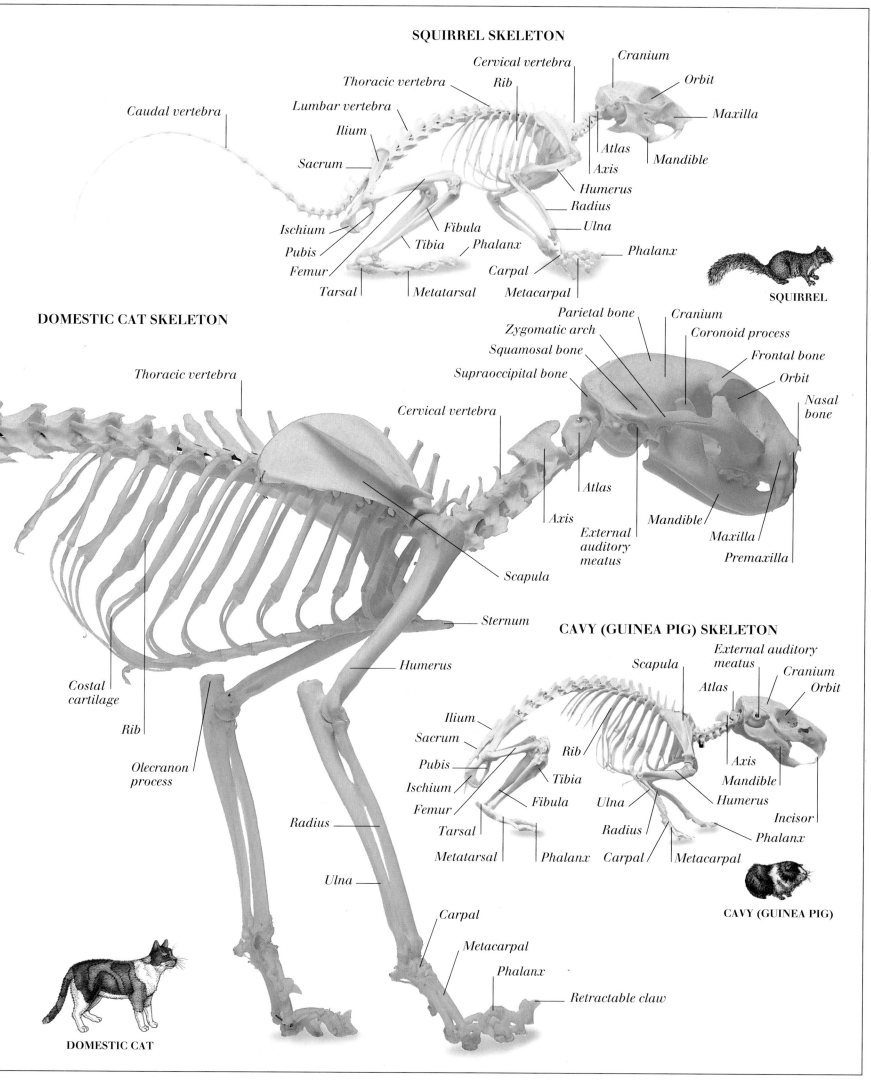

SQUIRREL SKELETON

Caudal vertebra

Thoracic vertebra

Lumbar vertebra

Cervical vertebra

Rib

Cranium

Orbit

Maxilla

Ilium

Atlas

Mandible

Sacrum

Axis

Humerus

Radius

Ischium

Ulna

Fibula

Phalanx

Phalanx

Pubis

Tibia

Carpal

Femur

Tarsal

Metatarsal

Metacarpal

SQUIRREL

DOMESTIC CAT SKELETON

Parietal bone

Cranium

Zygomatic arch

Coronoid process

Squamosal bone

Frontal bone

Thoracic vertebra

Supraoccipital bone

Orbit

Cervical vertebra

Nasal bone

Atlas

Axis

Mandible

Scapula

Maxilla

External auditory meatus

Premaxilla

Sternum

CAVY (GUINEA PIG) SKELETON

Humerus

External auditory meatus

Scapula

Cranium

Atlas

Orbit

Costal cartilage

Ilium

Rib

Rib

Sacrum

Axis

Pubis

Tibia

Mandible

Olecranon process

Ischium

Humerus

Femur

Fibula

Ulna

Incisor

Radius

Tarsal

Phalanx

Radius

Metatarsal

Phalanx

Carpal

Metacarpal

Ulna

CAVY (GUINEA PIG)

Carpal

Metacarpal

Phalanx

Retractable claw

DOMESTIC CAT

35

Land mammal skeletons 2

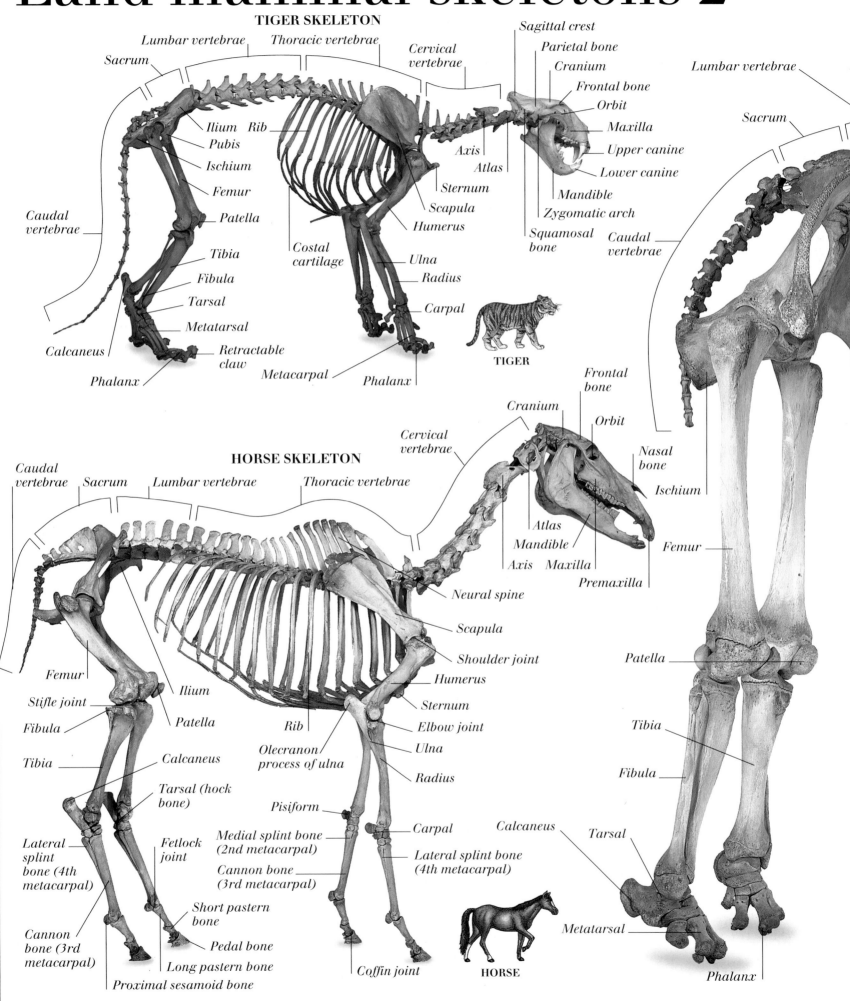

TIGER SKELETON

Lumbar vertebrae
Thoracic vertebrae
Cervical vertebrae
Sagittal crest
Parietal bone
Cranium
Frontal bone
Orbit
Maxilla
Upper canine
Lower canine
Mandible
Zygomatic arch
Squamosal bone
Sacrum
Ilium
Rib
Pubis
Ischium
Femur
Axis
Atlas
Sternum
Scapula
Humerus
Patella
Caudal vertebrae
Costal cartilage
Ulna
Radius
Tibia
Fibula
Tarsal
Carpal
Metatarsal
Calcaneus
Retractable claw
Metacarpal
Phalanx
Phalanx

TIGER

Lumbar vertebrae
Sacrum
Caudal vertebrae
Frontal bone
Cranium
Orbit
Cervical vertebrae
Nasal bone
Ischium
Atlas
Mandible
Femur
Axis
Maxilla
Premaxilla
Patella
Tibia
Fibula

HORSE SKELETON

Caudal vertebrae
Sacrum
Lumbar vertebrae
Thoracic vertebrae
Neural spine
Scapula
Shoulder joint
Humerus
Sternum
Elbow joint
Ulna
Radius
Femur
Stifle joint
Fibula
Ilium
Patella
Rib
Tibia
Calcaneus
Olecranon process of ulna
Pisiform
Tarsal (hock bone)
Carpal
Medial splint bone (2nd metacarpal)
Lateral splint bone (4th metacarpal)
Calcaneus
Tarsal
Lateral splint bone (4th metacarpal)
Fetlock joint
Cannon bone (3rd metacarpal)
Short pastern bone
Cannon bone (3rd metacarpal)
Pedal bone
Long pastern bone
Coffin joint
Metatarsal
Proximal sesamoid bone
Phalanx

HORSE

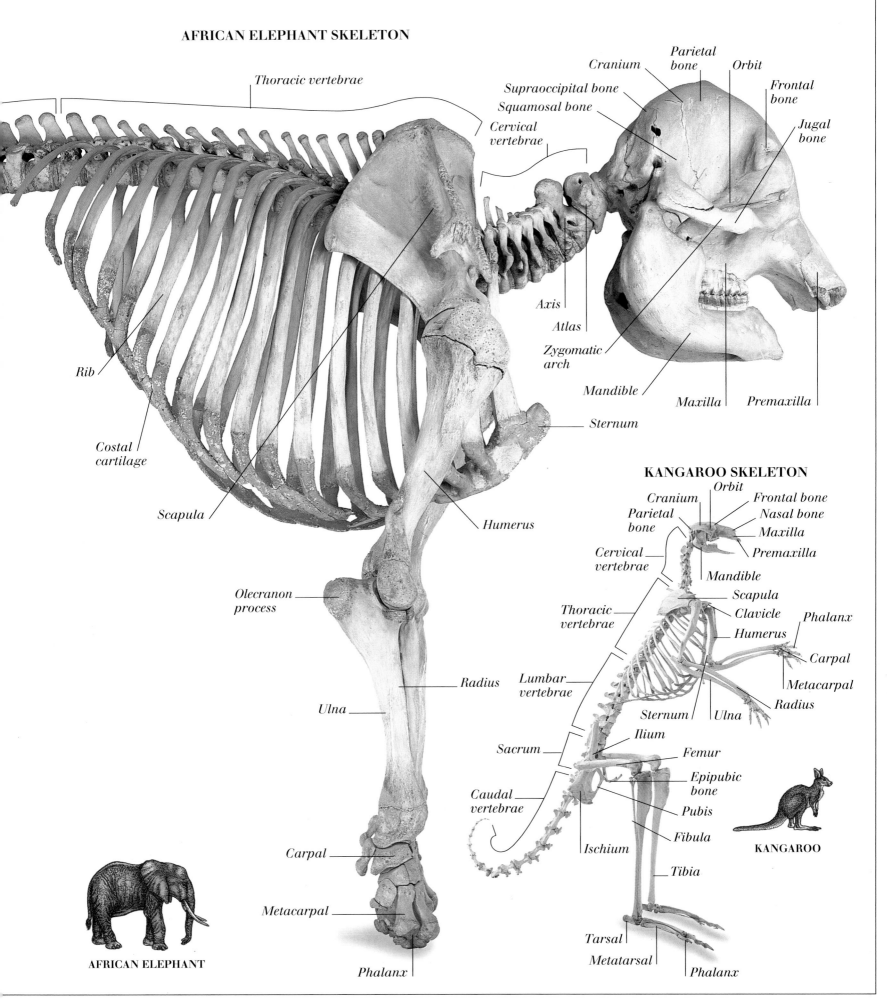

AFRICAN ELEPHANT SKELETON

Thoracic vertebrae

Cranium

Parietal bone

Orbit

Supraoccipital bone

Frontal bone

Squamosal bone

Jugal bone

Cervical vertebrae

Axis

Atlas

Zygomatic arch

Mandible

Maxilla

Premaxilla

Rib

Sternum

Costal cartilage

Scapula

Humerus

KANGAROO SKELETON

Orbit

Cranium

Frontal bone

Parietal bone

Nasal bone

Maxilla

Premaxilla

Cervical vertebrae

Mandible

Scapula

Clavicle

Phalanx

Thoracic vertebrae

Humerus

Carpal

Metacarpal

Radius

Olecranon process

Lumbar vertebrae

Sternum

Ulna

Radius

Ulna

Ilium

Femur

Sacrum

Epipubic bone

Caudal vertebrae

Pubis

Fibula

KANGAROO

Ischium

Carpal

Tibia

Metacarpal

Tarsal

Metatarsal

Phalanx

AFRICAN ELEPHANT

Phalanx

Early human relatives

THE DEVELOPMENT OF the modern human skeleton has involved changes associated with the shift from a quadrupedal (four-footed) stance to an upright, bipedal (two-footed) stance, and also with an enlarging cranium. Ape-like *Proconsul africanus*, which lived 20 million years ago, had the long pelvis and arms typical of a quadrupedal stance. However, hominid fossil remains from 5 million years ago have strong leg bones, a broad pelvis, and an S-shaped backbone, suggesting a bipedal stance. These features can be seen in 3-million-year-old *Australopithecus afarensis* ("Lucy"), and also in later skeletons, such as those of *Homo erectus* (Upright Man), *Homo neanderthalensis* (Neanderthal Man), and *Homo sapiens* (modern human). However, *Homo sapiens* has a larger brain than its ancestors, with a smaller face and jaw. All whole skeletons and external views shown here are reconstructions.

HOMO
NEANDERTHALENSIS
CRANIUM

AUSTRALOPITHECUS AFARENSIS ("LUCY")

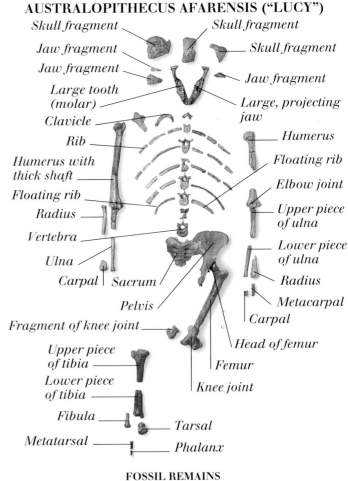

Skull fragment
Skull fragment
Skull fragment
Jaw fragment
Jaw fragment
Jaw fragment
Large tooth (molar)
Large, projecting jaw
Clavicle
Humerus
Rib
Floating rib
Humerus with thick shaft
Elbow joint
Floating rib
Upper piece of ulna
Radius
Vertebra
Lower piece of ulna
Ulna
Radius
Carpal   Sacrum
Metacarpal
Pelvis
Carpal
Fragment of knee joint
Head of femur
Upper piece of tibia
Femur
Lower piece of tibia
Knee joint
Fibula
Tarsal
Metatarsal
Phalanx

FOSSIL REMAINS

PROCONSUL AFRICANUS

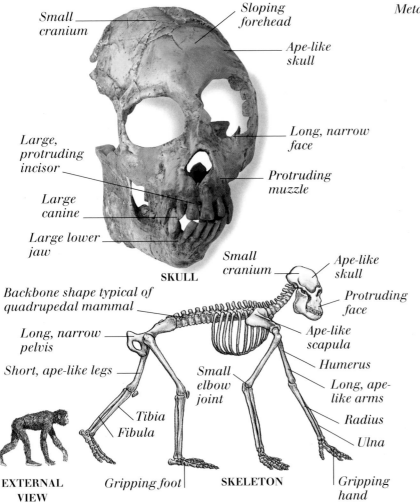

Small cranium
Sloping forehead
Ape-like skull
Large, protruding incisor
Long, narrow face
Large canine
Protruding muzzle
Large lower jaw

SKULL

Backbone shape typical of quadrupedal mammal
Small cranium
Ape-like skull
Long, narrow pelvis
Protruding face
Short, ape-like legs
Ape-like scapula
Small elbow joint
Humerus
Tibia
Fibula
Long, ape-like arms
Radius
Ulna

EXTERNAL VIEW
Gripping foot
SKELETON
Gripping hand

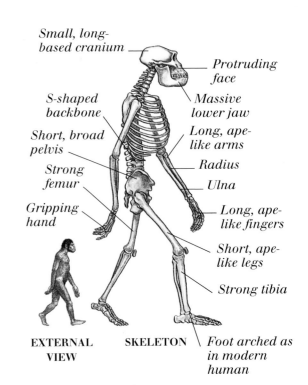

Small, long-based cranium
Protruding face
S-shaped backbone
Massive lower jaw
Short, broad pelvis
Long, ape-like arms
Strong femur
Radius
Gripping hand
Ulna
Long, ape-like fingers
Short, ape-like legs
Strong tibia

EXTERNAL VIEW
SKELETON
Foot arched as in modern human

HOMO ERECTUS

Sloping forehead

Smaller cranium

Thick skull

Prominent supraorbital ridge

Wide-set eyes

Deep, flat cheek-bone

Broad, flat nose

Wide face

SKULL

HOMO NEANDERTHALENSIS

Large, flat-topped cranium

Thinner skull

Prominent supraorbital ridge

Sloping forehead

Domed forehead

Close-set eyes

Long face

Hard, strong teeth

Large mandible

No chin (mandibular protuberance)

SKULL

HOMO SAPIENS

Rounded cranium

Thin skull

Domed forehead

Wide-set eyes

Hard, strong teeth

Small mandible

More prominent chin (mandibular protuberance)

SKULL

Small, long-based cranium

Slightly protruding face

Scapula

Rib

S-shaped backbone

Radius

Short, broad pelvis

Ulna

Femur

Long, thick tibia

Long legs

Long fibula

EXTERNAL VIEW

SKELETON

Prominent supraorbital ridge

Low, flat-topped, short-based cranium

Less prominent cheek-bones

Scapula

Large mandible

Thick-shafted humerus

Large elbow joint

Rib

Radius

S-shaped backbone

Ulna

Short, broad pelvis

Long thumb

Gripping hand

Short, thick tibia

Thick, curved femur

Short fibula

Large ankle joint

EXTERNAL VIEW

SKELETON

Reduced supraorbital ridge

Domed forehead

Large, short-based cranium

Small mandible

Scapula

Flat face

Humerus

Rib

S-shaped backbone

Ulna

Radius

Short, broad pelvis

Opposable thumb

Long femur

Long tibia

Long fibula

EXTERNAL VIEW

SKELETON

39

Bone structure and function

LIVING BONE IS A HARD, constantly changing, self-repairing tissue that is supplied with blood vessels and nerves. It consists of bone cells and the intercellular matrix that lies between them. About 65 per cent of this matrix consists of mineral salts, mainly calcium phosphate, that give bone its hardness; the other 35 per cent consists mainly of collagen fibres that provide flexibility. Bones have a thin outer coat of periosteum which contains osteoblasts (bone-forming cells) and osteoclasts (bone-destroying cells). Within the periosteum is a layer of compact bone that consists of concentric cylinders (lamellae) of matrix called osteons (Haversian systems) each of which acts as a weight-bearing pillar. Osteons are laid down around a central (Haversian) canal, which contains the blood vessels that supply osteocytes (mature bone cells) with nutrients and oxygen; Volkmann's canals connect adjacent Haversian canals. Bone matrix is maintained by osteocytes, which are found in lacunae (chambers) at the junctions of lamellae. Osteocytes communicate through dendrites (cell processes) that pass along tiny canals known as canaliculi. Spongy (cancellous) bone is situated within compact bone and consists of struts (trabeculae) that make it both light and strong. Red bone marrow, found in the spaces within cancellous bone, produces red and white blood cells.

MICROGRAPH OF LAMELLA FRAGMENT

Bone matrix

Layers of collagen fibres and mineral salts

Lamella (layer of bone)

Crystallites aligned parallel to collagen fibres

MICROGRAPH OF SPONGY BONE

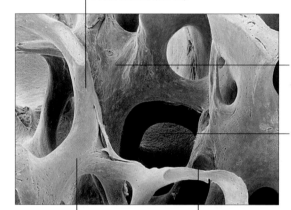

Trabecula (strut)

Trabecular plate

Marrow space

Bifurcation

Trabecular bar

MICROGRAPH OF OSTEON

Blood vessels, nerves, and lymphatic vessels in Haversian canal

Lacuna

Lamella

Osteon

Lacuna

STRUCTURAL FEATURES OF BONE

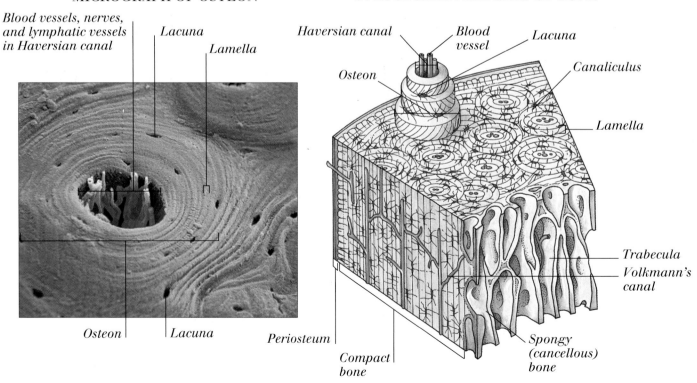

Haversian canal

Blood vessel

Lacuna

Osteon

Canaliculus

Lamella

Trabecula

Volkmann's canal

Periosteum

Compact bone

Spongy (cancellous) bone

MICROGRAPH OF OSTEOCYTE IN LACUNA

MICROGRAPH OF OSTEOCLAST

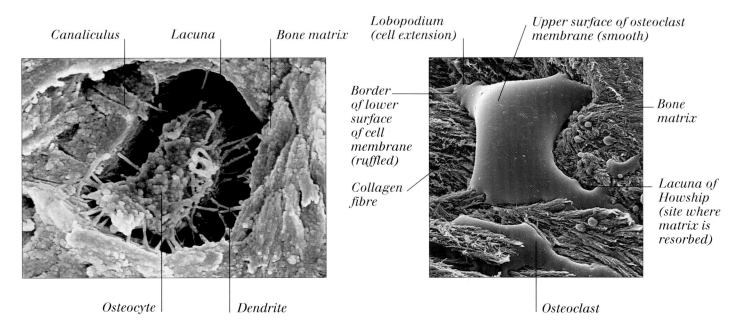

Canaliculus — Lacuna — Bone matrix

Osteocyte — Dendrite

Lobopodium (cell extension) — Upper surface of osteoclast membrane (smooth)

Border of lower surface of cell membrane (ruffled) — Collagen fibre

Bone matrix

Lacuna of Howship (site where matrix is resorbed)

Osteoclast

MICROGRAPH OF RED BONE MARROW

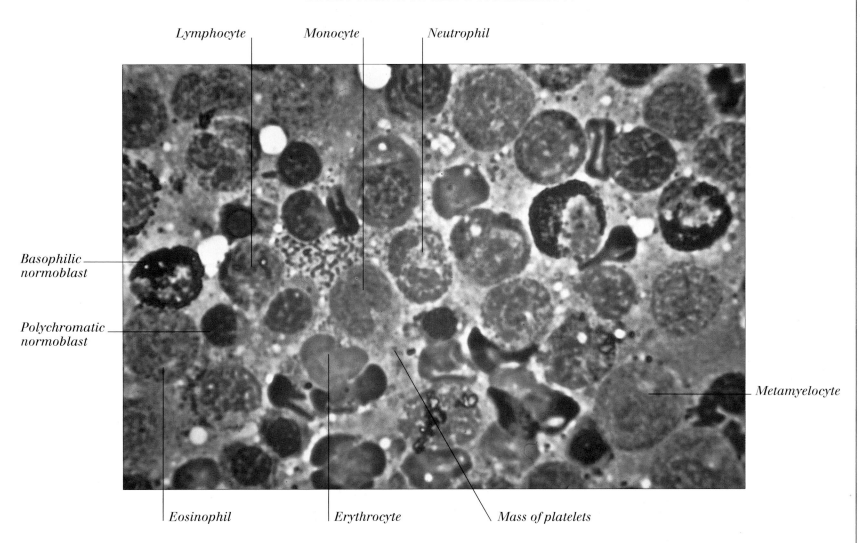

Lymphocyte — Monocyte — Neutrophil

Basophilic normoblast

Polychromatic normoblast

Metamyelocyte

Eosinophil — Erythrocyte — Mass of platelets

Joints

SUTURES OF SKULL

A JOINT IS A SITE where two or more bones meet. Joints have two main functions: to allow movement, and to maintain stability. Tough, inelastic ligaments prevent joint dislocation. There are three types of joints: immobile fibrous joints, such as the sutures between skull bones; slightly movable cartilaginous joints, such as those between vertebrae; and highly mobile synovial joints. Most body joints are synovial. To enable smooth movement, the ends of the bones of synovial joints are covered with glassy hyaline cartilage and separated by a cavity filled with synovial fluid. Five main types of synovial joints are found in mammals: pivot joints permit rotation of one bone against or inside another; ball-and-socket joints allow movement in all directions; hinge joints allow bending and straightening only; saddle joints permit backwards, forwards, and side-to-side movements; and plane joints allow short, gliding movements.

HIP JOINT LIGAMENTS

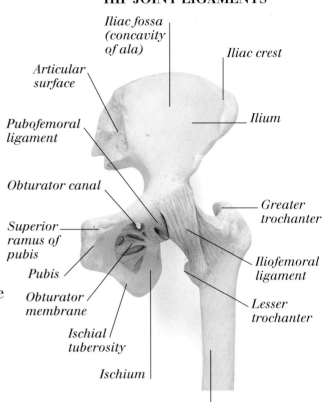

- Iliac fossa (concavity of ala)
- Iliac crest
- Articular surface
- Ilium
- Pubofemoral ligament
- Obturator canal
- Greater trochanter
- Superior ramus of pubis
- Iliofemoral ligament
- Pubis
- Obturator membrane
- Lesser trochanter
- Ischial tuberosity
- Ischium
- Femur

ANATOMY OF HIP JOINT

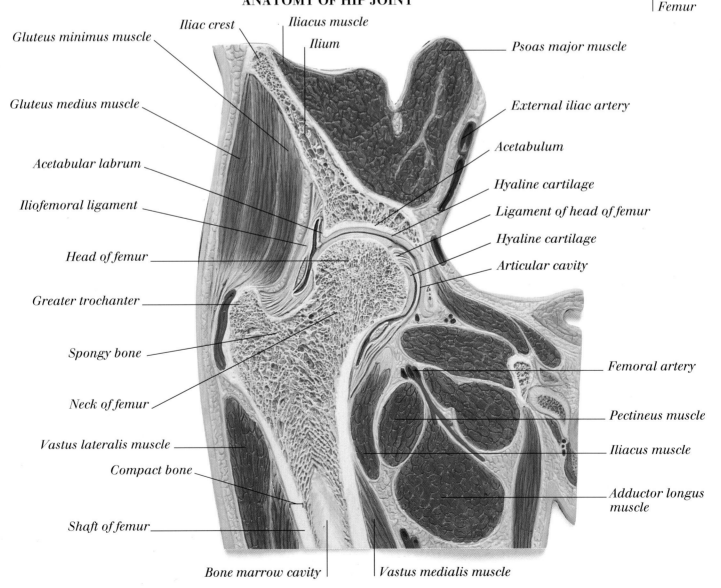

- Gluteus minimus muscle
- Iliac crest
- Iliacus muscle
- Ilium
- Psoas major muscle
- Gluteus medius muscle
- External iliac artery
- Acetabular labrum
- Acetabulum
- Iliofemoral ligament
- Hyaline cartilage
- Head of femur
- Ligament of head of femur
- Hyaline cartilage
- Greater trochanter
- Articular cavity
- Spongy bone
- Femoral artery
- Neck of femur
- Pectineus muscle
- Vastus lateralis muscle
- Iliacus muscle
- Compact bone
- Adductor longus muscle
- Shaft of femur
- Bone marrow cavity
- Vastus medialis muscle

TYPES OF SYNOVIAL JOINT

PIVOT JOINT

BALL-AND-SOCKET JOINT

SADDLE JOINT

HINGE JOINT

PLANE JOINT

JOINTS IN HUMAN

Temporomandibular joint

Sternoclavicular joint

Intervertebral joint

Shoulder (glenohumeral) joint

Vertebrocostal joint

Intervertebral joint

Elbow joint

Proximal radio-ulnar joint

Sacroiliac joint

Hip (coxal) joint

Carpometacarpal joint

Wrist (radiocarpal) joint

Carpometacarpal joint of first digit

Intercarpal joint

Pubic symphysis

Interphalangeal joint

Knee (tibiofemoral) joint

Knee (femoropatellar) joint

Proximal tibiofibular joint

Distal tibiofibular joint

Intertarsal joint

Ankle (talocrural) joint

Toe (interphalangeal) joint

JOINTS IN HARE

Intervertebral joint

Atlanto-axial joint

Vertebrocostal joint

Shoulder (glenohumeral) joint

Elbow joint

Knee (tibiofemoral) joint

Hip (coxal) joint

Intercarpal joint

Ankle (talocrural) joint

Intertarsal joint

Carpometacarpal joint

Interphalangeal joint

HARE

JOINTS IN PLATYPUS

Atlanto-axial joint

Interphalangeal joint

Interphalangeal joint

Intercarpal joint

Intercarpal joint

Shoulder (glenohumeral) joint

Vertebrocostal joint

Elbow joint

Knee (tibiofemoral) joint

Interphalangeal joint

Hip (coxal) joint

Intertarsal joint

PLATYPUS

Human skulls

THE BONES OF THE HUMAN SKULL serve several functions: the cranial bones surround and protect the brain, while the facial bones provide attachment points for facial muscles, as well as openings for eating and breathing, and cavities for the sensory organs. The facial bones also provide anchorage for the teeth. With the exception of the mandible (lower jaw) and the ear ossicles, the skull bones are knitted together by immovable joints called sutures. To allow blood vessels, nerves, and the spinal cord to pass through the skull, the skull bones are perforated by foramina (holes). The bone structure of early human skulls differs greatly from that of modern humans. The 200,000-year-old specimen of a *Homo heidelbergensis* skull (originally called "Rhodesian Man") has no forehead, prominent supraorbital (brow) ridges, and a large upper jaw. The skull of *Homo neanderthalensis* ("Neanderthal Man") – who lived 100,000 to 35,000 years ago and immediately preceded *Homo sapiens* (modern human) in Europe – had heavy supraorbital ridges and a sharply sloping forehead. In contrast, the skull of *Homo sapiens* has a more domed forehead, a flatter face, and a smaller jaw.

HOMO HEIDELBERGENSIS ("RHODESIAN MAN")

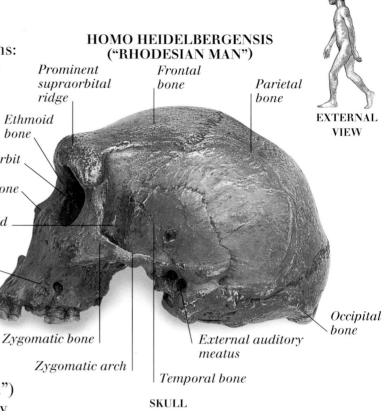

Prominent supraorbital ridge

Frontal bone

Parietal bone

Ethmoid bone

Orbit

Nasal bone

Sphenoid bone

Maxilla

Zygomatic bone

Zygomatic arch

External auditory meatus

Temporal bone

Occipital bone

EXTERNAL VIEW

SKULL

HOMO NEANDERTHALENSIS

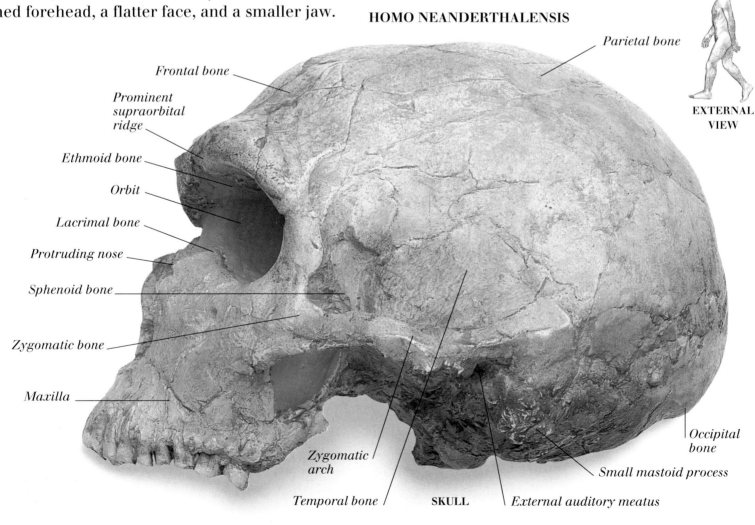

Frontal bone

Prominent supraorbital ridge

Ethmoid bone

Orbit

Lacrimal bone

Protruding nose

Sphenoid bone

Zygomatic bone

Maxilla

Parietal bone

EXTERNAL VIEW

Zygomatic arch

Temporal bone

SKULL

External auditory meatus

Small mastoid process

Occipital bone

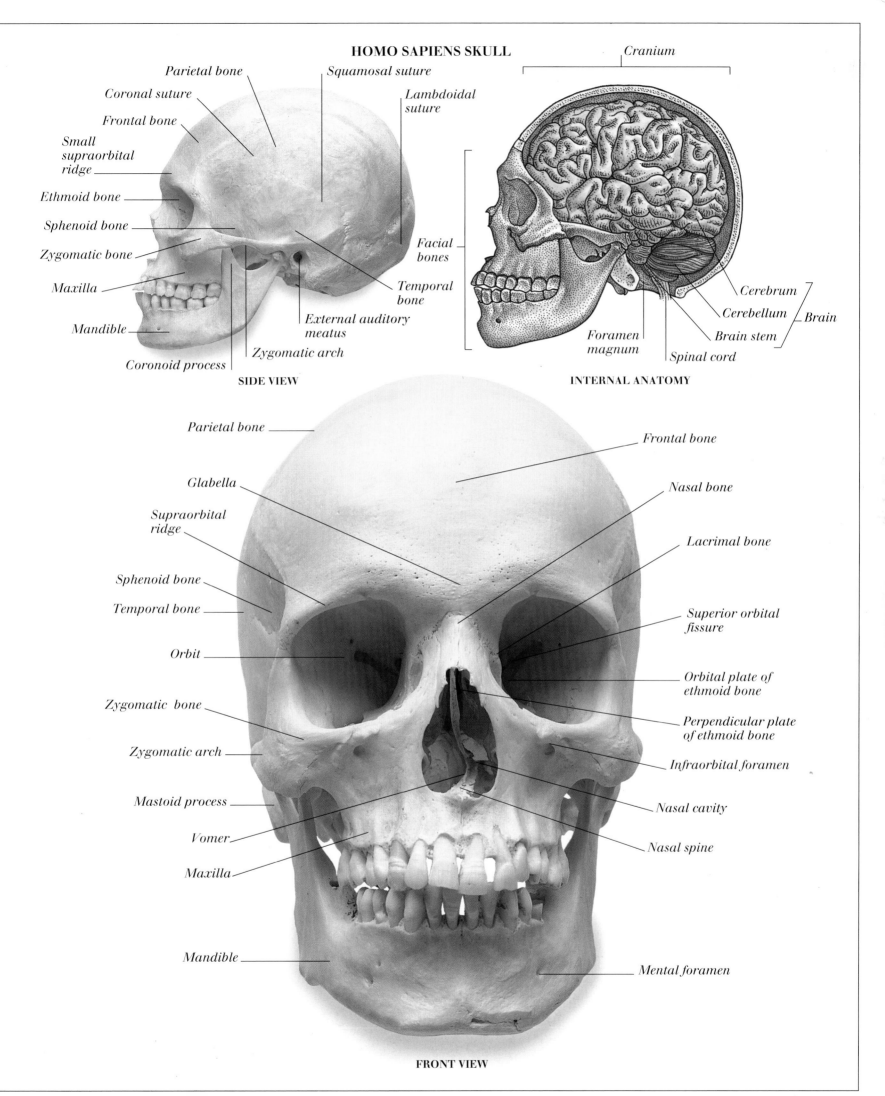

HOMO SAPIENS SKULL

Cranium

SIDE VIEW

Parietal bone
Coronal suture
Frontal bone
Small supraorbital ridge
Ethmoid bone
Sphenoid bone
Zygomatic bone
Maxilla
Mandible
Coronoid process
Zygomatic arch
External auditory meatus
Squamosal suture
Lambdoidal suture
Facial bones
Temporal bone

INTERNAL ANATOMY

Cerebrum
Cerebellum
Brain stem
Brain
Foramen magnum
Spinal cord

FRONT VIEW

Parietal bone
Glabella
Supraorbital ridge
Sphenoid bone
Temporal bone
Orbit
Zygomatic bone
Zygomatic arch
Mastoid process
Vomer
Maxilla
Mandible
Frontal bone
Nasal bone
Lacrimal bone
Superior orbital fissure
Orbital plate of ethmoid bone
Perpendicular plate of ethmoid bone
Infraorbital foramen
Nasal cavity
Nasal spine
Mental foramen

Animal skulls

ALL VERTEBRATES HAVE A skull made of fused bones and a movable mandible (lower jaw). The function of the skull is to house and protect the brain and sensory organs, and to allow eating and breathing. Each species of animal has a skull shape adapted to its particular lifestyle. Typically, birds, such as vultures, have lightweight skulls; carnivores (meat eaters), such as lions and crocodiles, have powerful jaws with sharp teeth; the toothless anteater has a long snout that enables it to probe into ant nests for food; and herbivores (plant eaters), such as the goat, have a loose-fitting lower jaw that permits side-to-side movement for grinding food. The two main muscles involved in biting and chewing are the temporalis and the masseter. In carnivores, both these muscles move the lower jaw up and down with a scissor-like action. In herbivores, the temporalis is relatively weak and the masseter provides the force needed to grind tough vegetation.

KING VULTURE SKULL

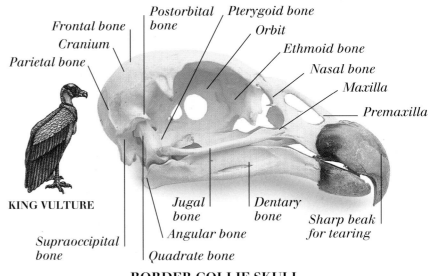

Frontal bone
Postorbital bone
Pterygoid bone
Cranium
Orbit
Parietal bone
Ethmoid bone
Nasal bone
Maxilla
Premaxilla
Jugal bone
Dentary bone
Sharp beak for tearing
Angular bone
Supraoccipital bone
Quadrate bone

KING VULTURE

BORDER COLLIE SKULL

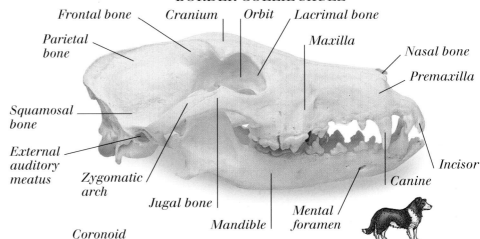

Frontal bone
Cranium
Orbit
Lacrimal bone
Parietal bone
Maxilla
Nasal bone
Premaxilla
Squamosal bone
External auditory meatus
Zygomatic arch
Jugal bone
Mandible
Mental foramen
Incisor
Canine

BORDER COLLIE

LION SKULL

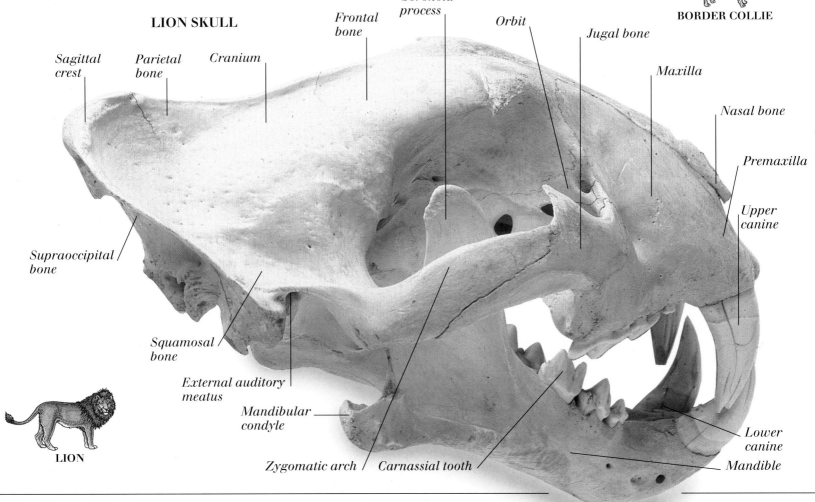

Sagittal crest
Parietal bone
Cranium
Frontal bone
Coronoid process
Orbit
Jugal bone
Maxilla
Nasal bone
Premaxilla
Upper canine
Supraoccipital bone
Squamosal bone
External auditory meatus
Mandibular condyle
Zygomatic arch
Carnassial tooth
Lower canine
Mandible

LION

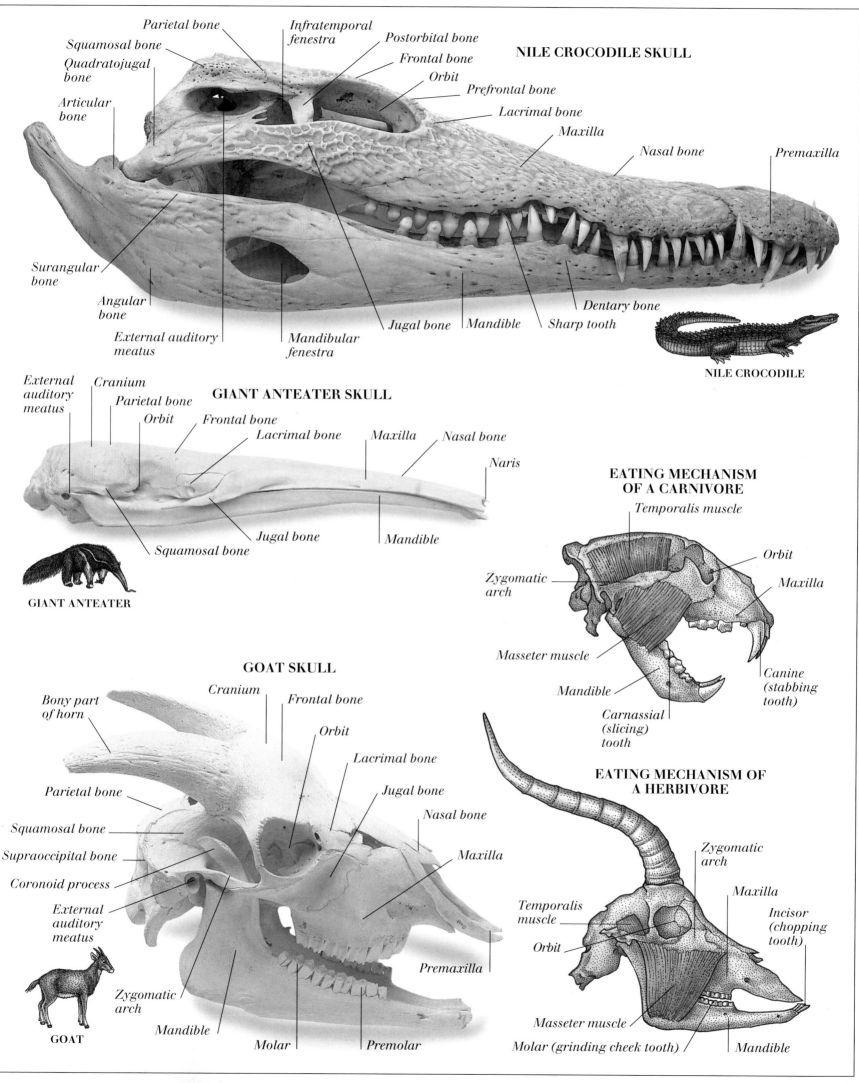

NILE CROCODILE SKULL

Parietal bone
Squamosal bone
Quadratojugal bone
Articular bone
Infratemporal fenestra
Postorbital bone
Frontal bone
Orbit
Prefrontal bone
Lacrimal bone
Maxilla
Nasal bone
Premaxilla
Surangular bone
Angular bone
External auditory meatus
Mandibular fenestra
Jugal bone
Mandible
Dentary bone
Sharp tooth

NILE CROCODILE

GIANT ANTEATER SKULL

External auditory meatus
Cranium
Parietal bone
Orbit
Frontal bone
Lacrimal bone
Maxilla
Nasal bone
Naris
Jugal bone
Squamosal bone
Mandible

GIANT ANTEATER

EATING MECHANISM OF A CARNIVORE

Temporalis muscle
Orbit
Zygomatic arch
Maxilla
Masseter muscle
Mandible
Canine (stabbing tooth)
Carnassial (slicing) tooth

GOAT SKULL

Bony part of horn
Cranium
Frontal bone
Orbit
Parietal bone
Lacrimal bone
Jugal bone
Squamosal bone
Nasal bone
Supraoccipital bone
Maxilla
Coronoid process
External auditory meatus
Premaxilla
Zygomatic arch
Mandible
Molar
Premolar

GOAT

EATING MECHANISM OF A HERBIVORE

Zygomatic arch
Maxilla
Incisor (chopping tooth)
Temporalis muscle
Orbit
Masseter muscle
Molar (grinding cheek tooth)
Mandible

47

Backbone

ALL VERTEBRATES HAVE A BACKBONE (vertebral column), which acts like a girder carrying the weight of the organs of the body. The backbone consists of a row of vertebrae separated by cartilaginous intervertebral discs that give limited flexibility. These vertebrae also form a protective tunnel around the spinal cord, while the neural spine and transverse processes of the vertebrae provide attachment points for muscles and ligaments. There are five types of vertebrae: cervical (neck), thoracic (chest), lumbar (abdominal), sacral (anchoring the backbone to the pelvis), and caudal (tail). Unlike most other vertebrates, birds have inflexible backbones – although the neck is flexible – to provide stability in flight. Most mammalian backbones (such as the hare's) curve upwards to help resist the downward pull of body weight, and vertebrae increase in size towards the lumbar end where stress is greatest. The human backbone is adapted to supporting the body in an upright position: it has an S-shaped curve that serves to position the body directly over the legs and feet.

ANATOMY OF HUMAN SPINAL COLUMN

Dorsal root ganglion

White matter

Central canal

Grey matter

Superior articular process

Ventral root of spinal nerve

Transverse process

Spinal cord

Spinal nerve

Neural spine

Intervertebral disc

Centrum

Dorsal root of spinal nerve

REAR VIEW

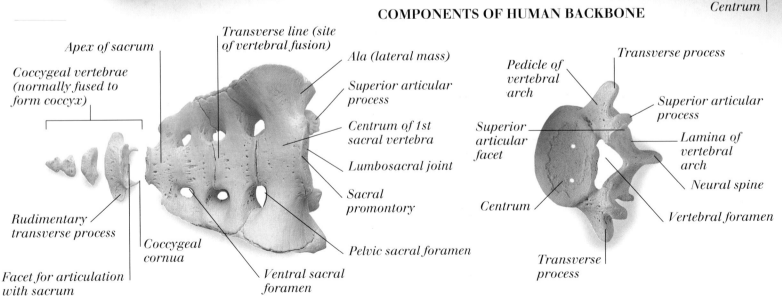

Lumbar vertebrae

Sacrum

Coccyx

Inferior articular process

Superior articular process

Centrum

COMPONENTS OF HUMAN BACKBONE

Apex of sacrum

Transverse line (site of vertebral fusion)

Ala (lateral mass)

Coccygeal vertebrae (normally fused to form coccyx)

Superior articular process

Centrum of 1st sacral vertebra

Lumbosacral joint

Sacral promontory

Rudimentary transverse process

Coccygeal cornua

Pelvic sacral foramen

Facet for articulation with sacrum

Ventral sacral foramen

Pedicle of vertebral arch

Transverse process

Superior articular process

Superior articular facet

Lamina of vertebral arch

Neural spine

Centrum

Vertebral foramen

Transverse process

FRONT VIEW OF SACRUM AND COCCYGEAL VERTEBRAE

TOP VIEW OF LUMBAR VERTEBRA

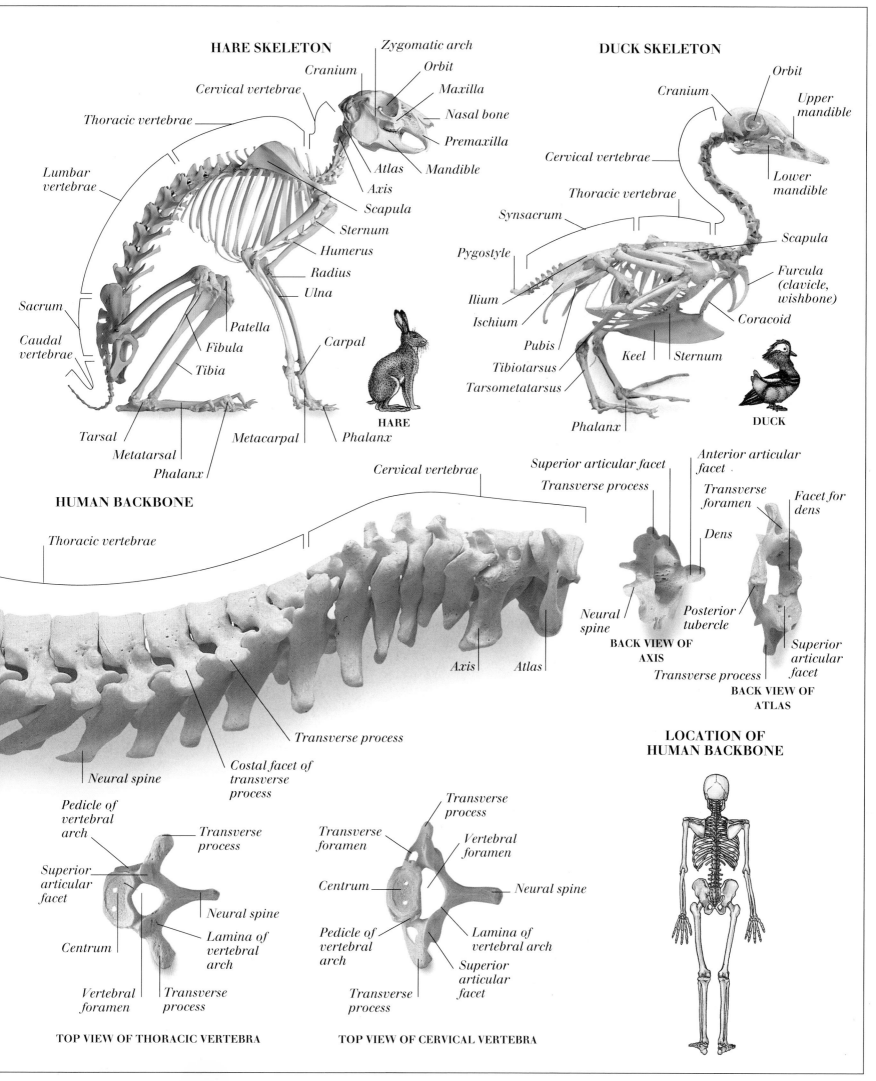

HARE SKELETON

Zygomatic arch

Cranium

Orbit

Cervical vertebrae

Maxilla

Thoracic vertebrae

Nasal bone

Premaxilla

Lumbar vertebrae

Atlas

Mandible

Axis

Scapula

Sternum

Humerus

Radius

Ulna

Sacrum

Caudal vertebrae

Patella

Fibula

Carpal

Tibia

Tarsal

Metatarsal

Phalanx

Metacarpal

Phalanx

HARE

DUCK SKELETON

Orbit

Cranium

Upper mandible

Cervical vertebrae

Lower mandible

Thoracic vertebrae

Synsacrum

Scapula

Pygostyle

Furcula (clavicle, wishbone)

Ilium

Coracoid

Ischium

Pubis

Keel

Sternum

Tibiotarsus

Tarsometatarsus

Phalanx

DUCK

HUMAN BACKBONE

Cervical vertebrae

Superior articular facet

Anterior articular facet

Transverse process

Transverse foramen

Facet for dens

Thoracic vertebrae

Dens

Neural spine

Posterior tubercle

Superior articular facet

Axis

Atlas

BACK VIEW OF AXIS

Transverse process

BACK VIEW OF ATLAS

Transverse process

Costal facet of transverse process

LOCATION OF HUMAN BACKBONE

Neural spine

Pedicle of vertebral arch

Transverse process

Transverse process

Superior articular facet

Transverse foramen

Vertebral foramen

Centrum

Centrum

Neural spine

Pedicle of vertebral arch

Lamina of vertebral arch

Neural spine

Lamina of vertebral arch

Vertebral foramen

Transverse process

Superior articular facet

Transverse process

TOP VIEW OF THORACIC VERTEBRA

TOP VIEW OF CERVICAL VERTEBRA

49

Ribcage

RIBS ARE CURVED, FLATTENED BONES found in all vertebrates. In land vertebrates, the ribs typically articulate with the thoracic vertebrae at one end and with the sternum (breastbone) at the other to form the ribcage. The ribcage protects the heart and lungs and is also flexible, allowing the lungs to inflate and deflate during breathing. Limbless vertebrates, such as snakes, have a tubular ribcage that supports the body and plays a part in locomotion. Humans have twelve pairs of ribs. Ribs 1–7, the true ribs, are attached to the sternum by costal cartilages. Ribs 8–12 are called the false ribs: ribs 8–10 are connected to one another by costal cartilage; ribs 11 and 12, the floating ribs, are connected only to the vertebral column. Breathing involves the action of the intercostal muscles (muscles between the ribs), and the diaphragm (the muscle sheet that separates the chest from the abdomen). When a person breathes in, the external intercostal muscles contract, moving the ribcage upwards and outwards, and the diaphragm contracts and flattens, drawing air into the lungs. When the person breathes out, the process is reversed, pushing air out of the lungs.

COBRA SKELETON

- Maxilla
- Cranium
- Mandible
- Vertebra
- Rib
- Articulation between rib and vertebra
- Caudal vertebra

COBRA

CHILLINGHAM BULL SKELETON

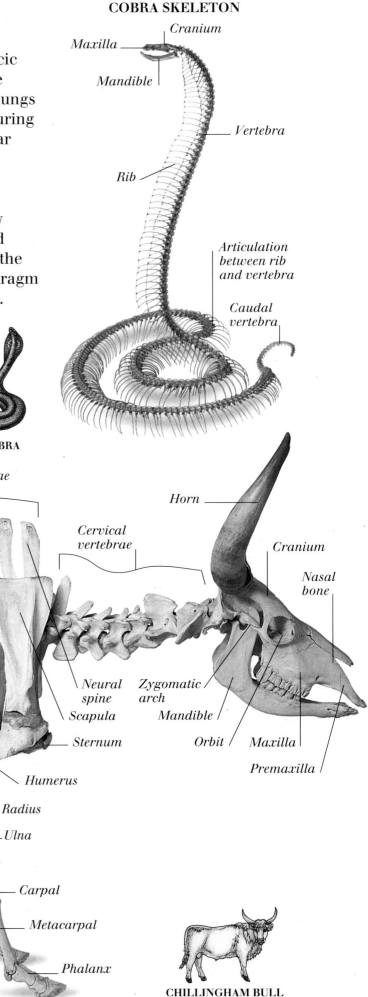

- Lumbar vertebrae
- Thoracic vertebrae
- Sacrum
- Cervical vertebrae
- Horn
- Caudal vertebrae
- Cranium
- Nasal bone
- Ilium
- Pubis
- Neural spine
- Zygomatic arch
- Scapula
- Mandible
- Ischium
- Sternum
- Orbit
- Maxilla
- Femur
- Patella
- Costal cartilage
- Humerus
- Premaxilla
- Tibia
- Rib
- Radius
- Calcaneus
- Olecranon process
- Ulna
- Tarsal
- Carpal
- Metatarsal
- Metacarpal
- Phalanx
- Phalanx

CHILLINGHAM BULL

HUMAN RIBCAGE

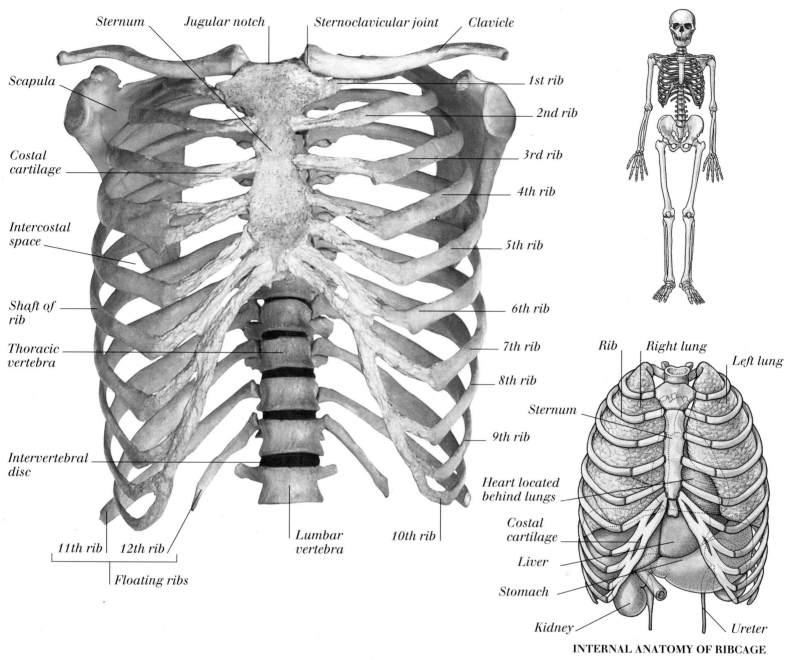

Sternum
Jugular notch
Sternoclavicular joint
Clavicle
Scapula
1st rib
2nd rib
Costal cartilage
3rd rib
4th rib
Intercostal space
5th rib
Shaft of rib
6th rib
Thoracic vertebra
7th rib
8th rib
Intervertebral disc
9th rib
11th rib
12th rib
Lumbar vertebra
10th rib
Floating ribs

LOCATION OF RIBCAGE

Rib
Right lung
Left lung
Sternum
Heart located behind lungs
Costal cartilage
Liver
Stomach
Kidney
Ureter

INTERNAL ANATOMY OF RIBCAGE

BREATHING MECHANISM

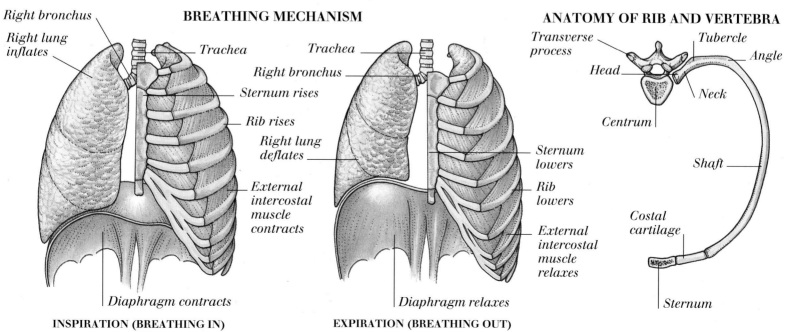

Right bronchus
Right lung inflates
Trachea
Sternum rises
Rib rises
External intercostal muscle contracts
Diaphragm contracts

INSPIRATION (BREATHING IN)

Trachea
Right bronchus
Right lung deflates
Sternum lowers
Rib lowers
External intercostal muscle relaxes
Diaphragm relaxes

EXPIRATION (BREATHING OUT)

ANATOMY OF RIB AND VERTEBRA

Transverse process
Tubercle
Angle
Head
Neck
Centrum
Shaft
Costal cartilage
Sternum

Pelvis

THE PELVIS CONSISTS OF TWO COXAE (known as the pelvic girdle), the sacrum, and the coccyx. Together, these bones connect the hind limbs to the backbone, transmit the force from the hind limbs to the rest of the body, and support and protect the organs of the lower abdomen. Each coxa is formed by the fusion of three bones: the ilium, ischium, and pubis. The coxae are joined at a cartilaginous joint known as the pubic symphysis. The joints between the coxae and the sacrum are called the sacroiliac joints. Four-legged animals, such as dogs and cattle, typically have a horizontally aligned, elongated pelvis. Chimpanzees, with their semi-upright posture, have an elongated, slightly tilted pelvis. In humans, who are fully upright, the pelvis is rounded and nearly vertical, so that the body is balanced directly over the feet.

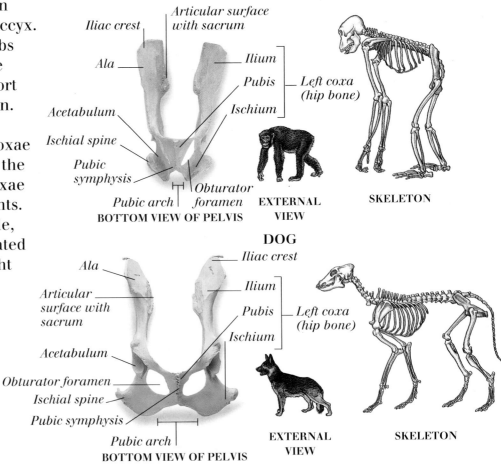

CHIMPANZEE

Iliac crest

Articular surface with sacrum

Ala

Ilium

Pubis

Left coxa (hip bone)

Ischium

Acetabulum

Ischial spine

Pubic symphysis

Obturator foramen

Pubic arch

BOTTOM VIEW OF PELVIS

EXTERNAL VIEW

SKELETON

DOG

Ala

Iliac crest

Articular surface with sacrum

Ilium

Pubis

Left coxa (hip bone)

Ischium

Acetabulum

Obturator foramen

Ischial spine

Pubic symphysis

Pubic arch

BOTTOM VIEW OF PELVIS

EXTERNAL VIEW

SKELETON

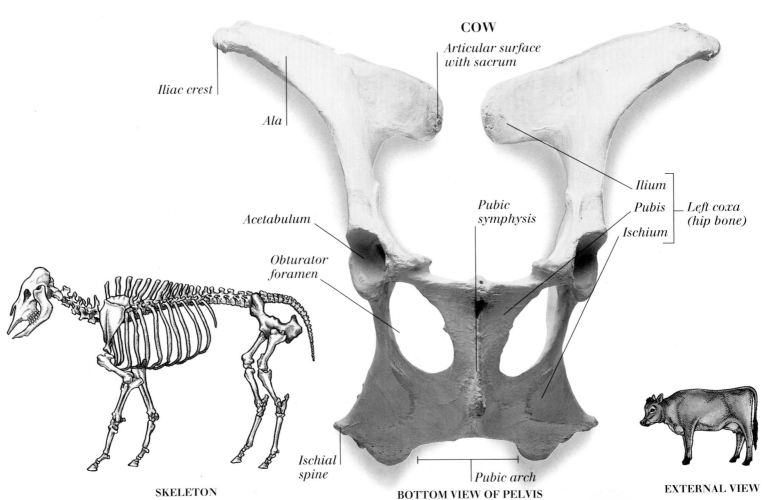

COW

Articular surface with sacrum

Iliac crest

Ala

Ilium

Pubic symphysis

Pubis

Left coxa (hip bone)

Ischium

Acetabulum

Obturator foramen

Ischial spine

Pubic arch

SKELETON

BOTTOM VIEW OF PELVIS

EXTERNAL VIEW

INTERNAL ANATOMY OF HUMAN PELVIS

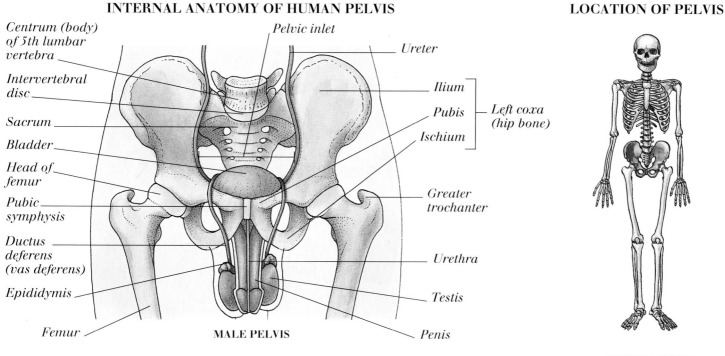

Centrum (body) of 5th lumbar vertebra

Pelvic inlet

Ureter

Intervertebral disc

Ilium

Pubis — *Left coxa (hip bone)*

Ischium

Sacrum

Bladder

Head of femur

Greater trochanter

Pubic symphysis

Ductus deferens (vas deferens)

Urethra

Epididymis

Testis

Femur

Penis

MALE PELVIS

LOCATION OF PELVIS

RIGHT COXA

Centrum (body) of 5th lumbar vertebra

Intervertebral disc

Uterus

Ureter

Fimbriae

Sacrum

Ovary

Ilium

Fallopian tube

Pubis — *Left coxa*

Ischium

Bladder

Greater trochanter

Head of femur

Urethra

Pubic symphysis

Femur

Vagina

FEMALE PELVIS

Anterior superior iliac spine

Iliac crest

Ala

Anterior inferior iliac spine

Ilium

Acetabulum

Posterior superior iliac spine

Greater sciatic notch

Pubic tubercle

Ischium

Pubis

Ischial tuberosity

Obturator foramen

SIDE VIEW

COMPARISON OF MALE AND FEMALE PELVISES

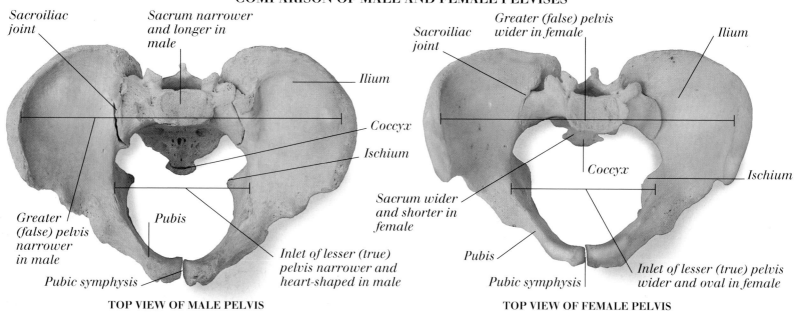

Sacroiliac joint

Sacrum narrower and longer in male

Greater (false) pelvis wider in female

Sacroiliac joint

Ilium

Ilium

Coccyx

Coccyx

Ischium

Ischium

Sacrum wider and shorter in female

Greater (false) pelvis narrower in male

Pubis

Inlet of lesser (true) pelvis narrower and heart-shaped in male

Pubis

Inlet of lesser (true) pelvis wider and oval in female

Pubic symphysis

Pubic symphysis

TOP VIEW OF MALE PELVIS

TOP VIEW OF FEMALE PELVIS

53

Forelimbs

THE FORELIMBS OF TETRAPODS (four-limbed vertebrates) are typically used for support, movement, and varying degrees of manipulation. They originated from an ancestral pentadactyl (five-fingered) forelimb. This would have consisted of a humerus (upper arm bone); an ulna and radius (lower arm bones); ten carpals (wrist bones); five metacarpals (palm bones); and five sets of phalanges (finger bones). During evolution, the number, shape, and size of the forelimb bones changed to adapt vertebrates to particular lifestyles. For example, the short, strong forelimbs of the armadillo are adapted for digging; the arm and finger bones of the sea lion form a broad flipper for swimming; the gibbon's long arm bones and elongated, gripping fingers provide a secure hold on branches; and in flying vertebrates, such as the rock dove and bat, the forelimbs have become wings. Some fast-moving mammals – for example, horses and ponies – stand on a hoofed third digit; this is an adaptation for speed. The human forelimb is adapted mainly for intricate manipulation rather than support or locomotion.

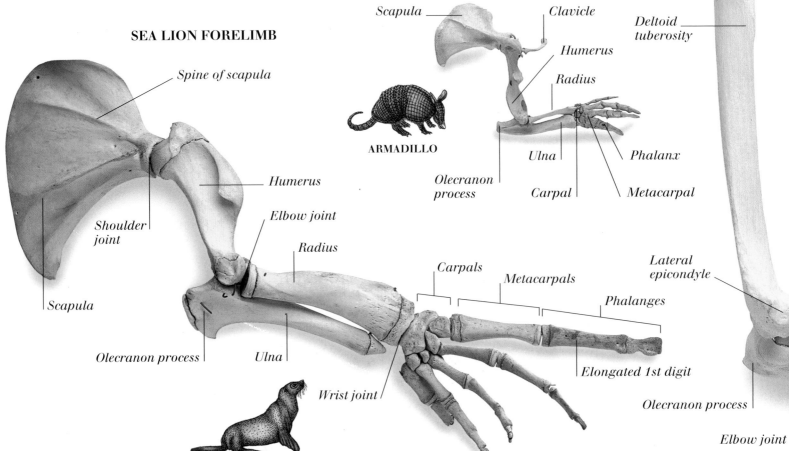

Spine of scapula

Acromion

Head of humerus

Coracoid process

Shoulder joint

Scapula

Humerus

Deltoid tuberosity

ARMADILLO FORELIMB

Scapula — *Clavicle*

Humerus

Radius

ARMADILLO

Ulna — *Phalanx*

Olecranon process

Carpal — *Metacarpal*

SEA LION FORELIMB

Spine of scapula

Humerus

Shoulder joint

Elbow joint

Radius

Carpals

Metacarpals

Lateral epicondyle

Phalanges

Scapula

Olecranon process

Ulna

Wrist joint

Elongated 1st digit

Olecranon process

Elbow joint

Radial tuberosity

SEA LION

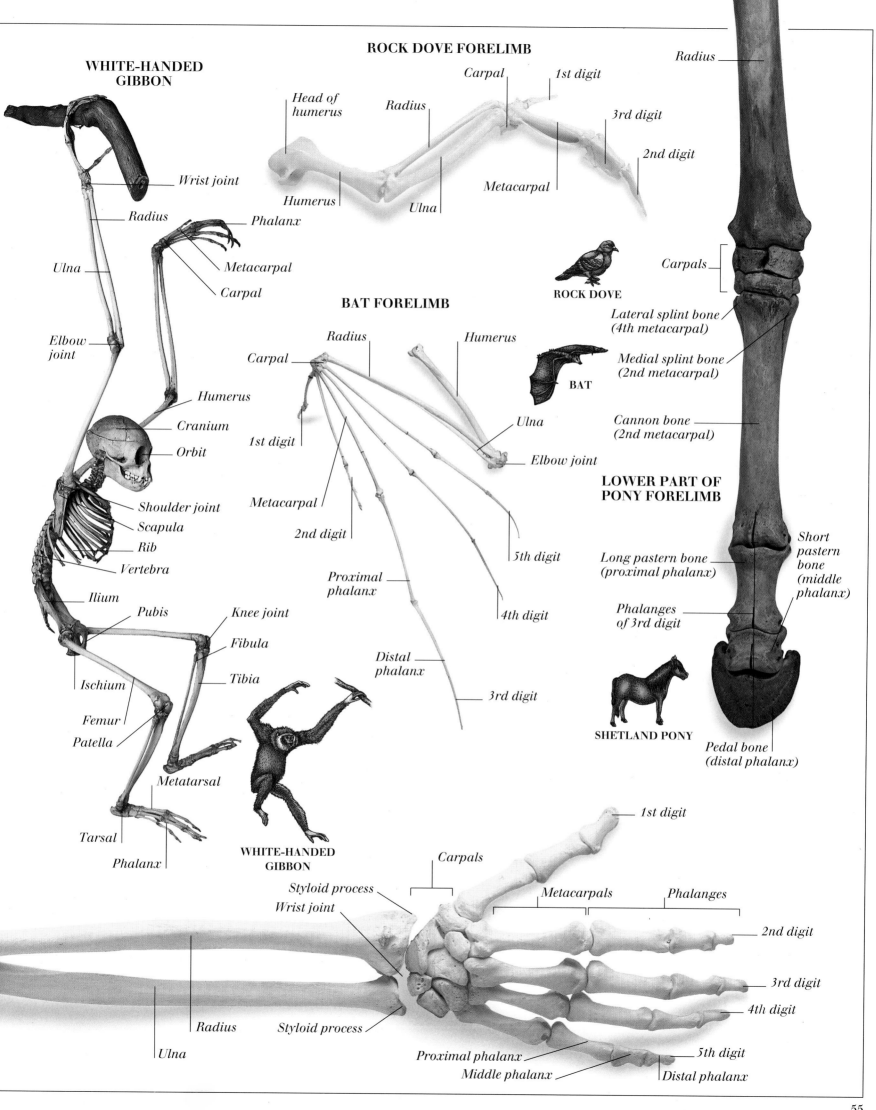

WHITE-HANDED GIBBON

Wrist joint
Radius
Phalanx
Metacarpal
Carpal
Ulna
Elbow joint
Humerus
Cranium
Orbit
Shoulder joint
Scapula
Rib
Vertebra
Ilium
Pubis
Knee joint
Fibula
Tibia
Ischium
Femur
Patella
Metatarsal
Tarsal
Phalanx

WHITE-HANDED GIBBON

ROCK DOVE FORELIMB

Head of humerus
Radius
Carpal
1st digit
3rd digit
2nd digit
Metacarpal
Humerus
Ulna

ROCK DOVE

BAT FORELIMB

Radius
Humerus
Carpal
1st digit
Metacarpal
2nd digit
5th digit
Proximal phalanx
4th digit
Distal phalanx
3rd digit
Ulna
Elbow joint

BAT

Radius

Carpals

Lateral splint bone (4th metacarpal)
Medial splint bone (2nd metacarpal)

Cannon bone (2nd metacarpal)

LOWER PART OF PONY FORELIMB

Long pastern bone (proximal phalanx)
Phalanges of 3rd digit
Short pastern bone (middle phalanx)
Pedal bone (distal phalanx)

SHETLAND PONY

Carpals
Styloid process
Wrist joint
Metacarpals
Phalanges
1st digit
2nd digit
3rd digit
4th digit
Radius
Styloid process
Ulna
Proximal phalanx
Middle phalanx
5th digit
Distal phalanx

Hind limbs

THE HIND LIMBS OF TETRAPODS (four-limbed vertebrates) are more powerful than the forelimbs, and generally provide most of the locomotive force. A typical hind limb consists of a femur (upper leg bone), a tibia and fibula (lower leg bones), tarsals (ankle bones), metatarsals (middle foot bones), and phalanges (toe bones). This arrangement, like that of tetrapod forelimbs, evolved from an ancestral pentadactyl (five-fingered) limb, and is adapted to fit particular lifestyles. The seal's short hind limb and elongated foot form a flipper that propels the animal through the water. Long leg and foot bones adapt the serval for pouncing, and the wallaby for balance and a powerful hopping action. The owl's strong hind limbs can be extended to seize prey; and the gibbon uses its long toes to grip branches. The hind limb of the ox has two hoof-tipped toes and fused metatarsals to give strength. The human leg is adapted for an upright posture: the leg bones are long and strong to support body weight, and the long, broad foot provides stability.

HUMAN HIND LIMB

Lateral epicondyle of femur

Patella

Knee joint

Lateral condyle of tibia

Tibial tuberosity

Tibia

Fibula

Ankle joint

Navicular

Intermediate cuneiform

Lateral cuneiform

Metatarsal

Digit

Phalanx

Cuboid

Talus

Calcaneus

GIBBON HIND LIMB

Head of femur

Femur

Patella

Knee joint

Fibula

Tibia

Metatarsal

Phalanx

Ankle joint

Calcaneus

SEAL HIND LIMB

SEAL

Femur

Tibia

Head of femur

Fibula

Tarsals

Metatarsals

Phalanges

WHITE-HANDED GIBBON

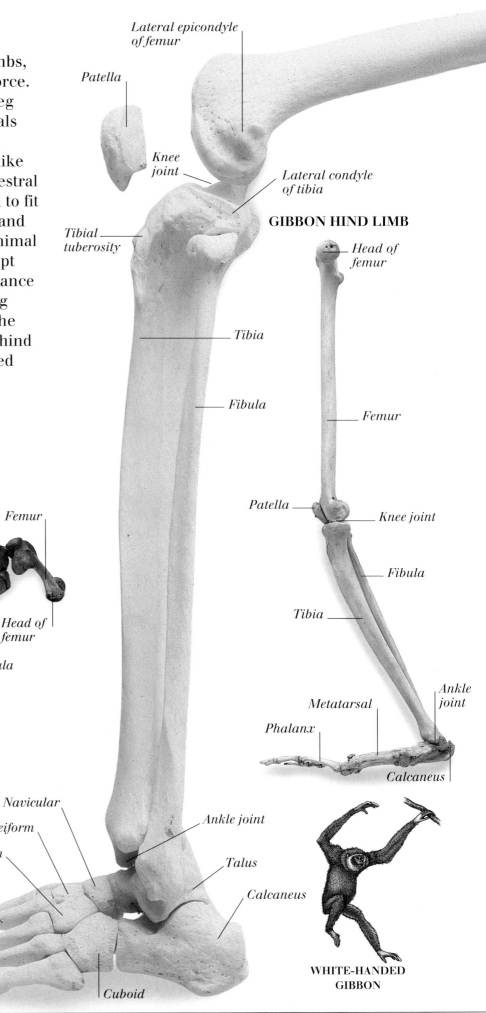

56

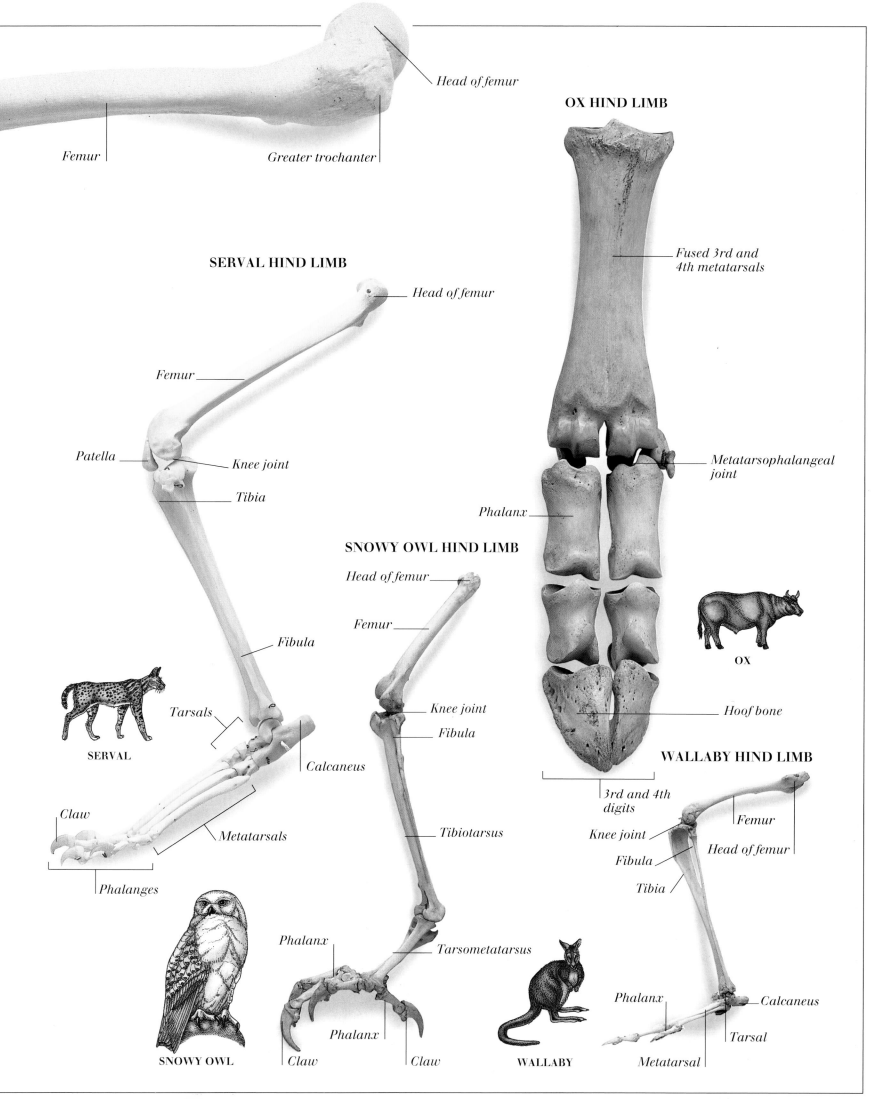

Femur

Head of femur

Greater trochanter

OX HIND LIMB

Fused 3rd and 4th metatarsals

SERVAL HIND LIMB

Head of femur

Femur

Patella

Knee joint

Tibia

Metatarsophalangeal joint

Phalanx

Fibula

SNOWY OWL HIND LIMB

Head of femur

Femur

Tarsals

SERVAL

Calcaneus

Knee joint

Fibula

OX

Claw

Metatarsals

Tibiotarsus

Hoof bone

Phalanges

WALLABY HIND LIMB

3rd and 4th digits

Knee joint

Femur

Fibula

Head of femur

Tibia

Phalanx

Tarsometatarsus

Phalanx

Calcaneus

Phalanx

Tarsal

SNOWY OWL

Claw

Claw

WALLABY

Metatarsal

57

Hands and feet

THE HANDS AND FEET of most tetrapods
(four-limbed vertebrates) are used for support
and movement. However, the human hand is adapted
for precise manipulation and grip. The skeleton of the
human hand consists of phalanges (finger bones),
metacarpals (palm bones), and carpals (wrist bones).
The first metacarpal and trapezium bone form
a highly mobile saddle joint that gives the
thumb its manoeuvrability. The human
foot acts as a lever to propel the body
forwards, aids balance, and provides
support. It consists of 26 bones: seven
tarsals (ankle bones), five metatarsals
(middle foot bones), and fourteen
phalanges (toe bones). The hands
and feet of other tetrapods are
adapted to their particular lifestyles:
the aye-aye's long fingers and toes
grip the branches of trees; the penguin's
wide foot provides balance and
stability on land; and the zebra's leg
rests on its third finger, increasing
agility and length of stride.

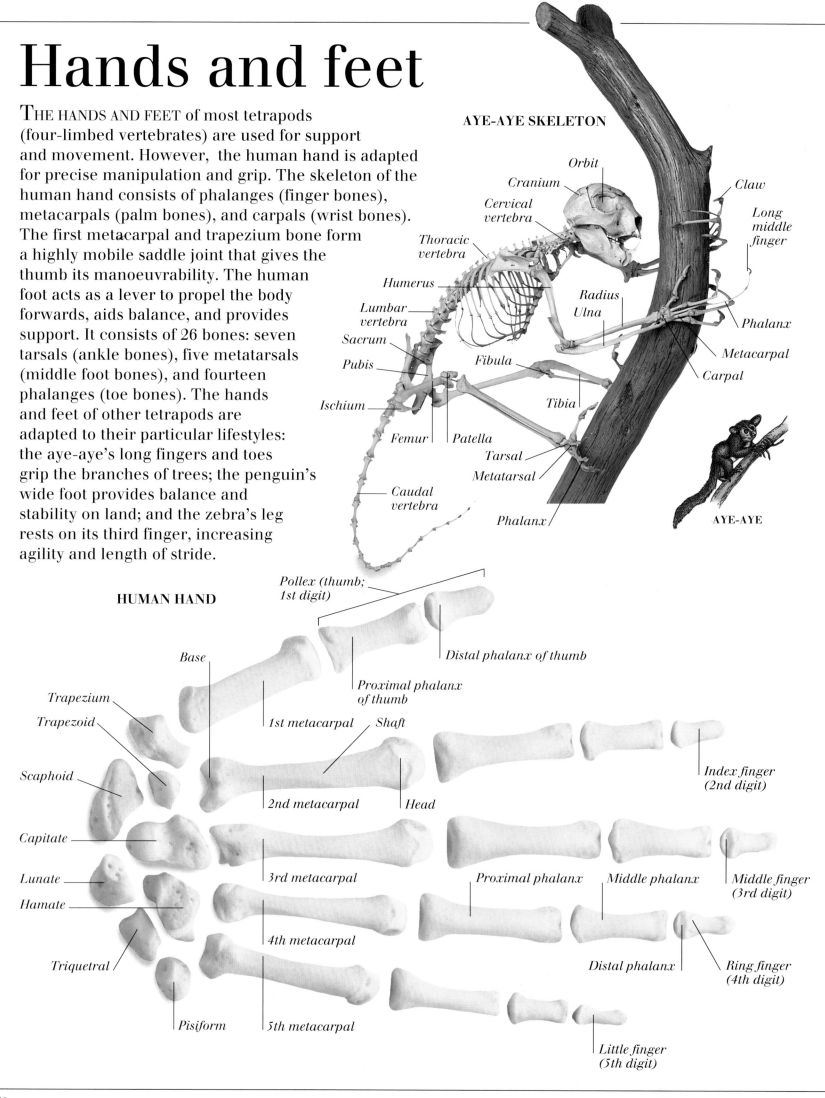

AYE-AYE SKELETON

Orbit

Cranium

Cervical
vertebra

Claw

Long
middle
finger

Thoracic
vertebra

Humerus

Radius

Ulna

Phalanx

Lumbar
vertebra

Metacarpal

Sacrum

Fibula

Carpal

Pubis

Ischium

Tibia

Femur

Patella

Tarsal

Metatarsal

Caudal
vertebra

Phalanx

AYE-AYE

HUMAN HAND

Pollex (thumb;
1st digit)

Base

Distal phalanx of thumb

Trapezium

Proximal phalanx
of thumb

Trapezoid

1st metacarpal

Shaft

Scaphoid

Index finger
(2nd digit)

2nd metacarpal

Head

Capitate

Lunate

3rd metacarpal

Proximal phalanx

Middle phalanx

Middle finger
(3rd digit)

Hamate

4th metacarpal

Triquetral

Distal phalanx

Ring finger
(4th digit)

Pisiform

5th metacarpal

Little finger
(5th digit)

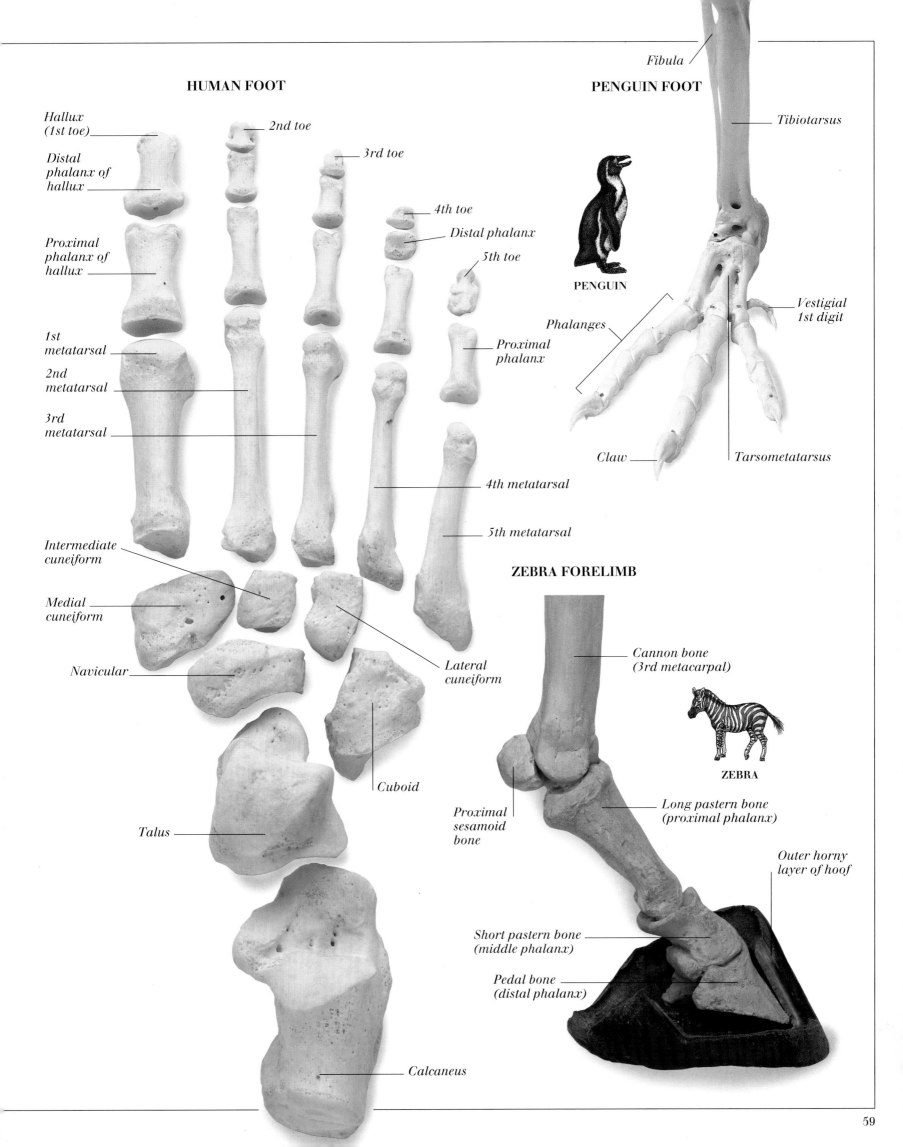

HUMAN FOOT

Hallux
(1st toe)

2nd toe

3rd toe

Distal
phalanx of
hallux

4th toe

Distal phalanx

Proximal
phalanx of
hallux

5th toe

1st
metatarsal

Proximal
phalanx

2nd
metatarsal

3rd
metatarsal

4th metatarsal

5th metatarsal

Intermediate
cuneiform

Medial
cuneiform

Navicular

Lateral
cuneiform

Cuboid

Talus

Calcaneus

PENGUIN FOOT

Fibula

Tibiotarsus

PENGUIN

Vestigial
1st digit

Phalanges

Claw

Tarsometatarsus

ZEBRA FORELIMB

Cannon bone
(3rd metacarpal)

ZEBRA

Long pastern bone
(proximal phalanx)

Proximal
sesamoid
bone

Outer horny
layer of hoof

Short pastern bone
(middle phalanx)

Pedal bone
(distal phalanx)

Index

60

Acknowledgments

Dorling Kindersley would like to thank:
Dr Chris Stringer, Dr Louise Humphrey, and Dr Peter Andrews at the Department of Palaeontology, The Natural History Museum, London; Dr Gary Sawyer and Dr Allison Andors of the American Museum of Natural History, New York; Martin Berry, Professor of Anatomy at Guy's Hospital, London for the loan of the human skeleton and the male and female pelvises; George Bridgeman at UMDS for permission to photograph the human skeleton and the male and female pelvises, pp12-15, 52-53; Brandon Broll at the Science Photo Library for editorial help and advice; Edward Bunting and Mary Lindsay for editorial help; Maureen Donovan for advice on labelling the bone marrow micrograph; Stephen Eeley, Jane Pickering, and the staff of

the Oxford University Museum for permission to photograph exhibits; Donald Farr at King's College, London, for editorial help and advice on pelvises; Darren Hill and Mark Wilde for additional design assistance.

Picture credits:
t top; *c* centre; *b* bottom; *l* left; *r* right.
The Publisher would like to thank the following for their kind permission to reproduce their photographs: Microscopix/ Andrew Syred 9cl, 16tr, 18tl, 40bl; Science Photo Library/ Scott Camazine 10bl,15t;/ Eric Grave 41b;/ Prof. P. Motta, Department of Anatomy, University La Sapienza, Rome front cover c,15bl,br, 40tr,cr, 41tl;/ David Scharf 41(tr)

Museum credits:
Dorling Kindersley would like to thank: The Natural History Museum, London; The University Museum, Oxford; The Royal Masonic Hospital, London; The University Museum of Zoology, Cambridge; Royal Scottish Museum, Edinburgh; Naturmuseum Senckenburg, Frankfurt.

Dorling Kindersley photographers:
Andy Crawford, Steve Gorton, Sarah Ashun

Makers or owners of models shown in this book: John Dunlop, prepared skeletons: Dogfish skeketon pp 22-23; Salamander skeleton pp 24-25; Monitor Lizard skeleton pp 28-29; Penguin skeleton p 31; Penguin foot p.59

 Somso Modelle, Coburg, Germany: section through buttercup root p.16; section through young woody stem p.17; model of skeleton p.21; hip joint with ligaments/anatomy of hip joint p.42

Additional illustrator: Elizabeth Gray (principal illustrators are credited separately on p.4)

Index: Kay Wright